OTHER BOOKS BY ROCHELLE OWENS

Rochelle Owens

New and Selected Poems
1961-1996

Junction Press
San Diego
1997

Some of these poems have appeared in the following magazines and anthologies: *Abacus, America a Prophecy, An Active Anthology, Another Chicago Magazine, A Big Jewish Book, Boundary 2, Broadway Boogie, A Century in Two Decades, The Coldspring Journal, Confrontation, Connections, Contact II, A Controversy of Poets, Damascus Road, Deep Down, First Intensity, Four Young Lady Poets, Intrepid, Moody Street Irregulars, New Wilderness Letter, NY Quarterly, Nimrod, No More Masks, Objects, Open Places, Open Poetry, The Partisan Review, Poetry Now, Poets On, Postmodern Culture, Psyche, Rising Tides, Shell, Six Pack, Some/Thing, Stations, Stooge, Sulfur, Sun, Talisman, Temblor, Texture, 13th Moon, Tree, Trobar, 2 plus 2, Unmuzzled Ox,* and *Zone.* The author wishes to express her gratitude to the following publishers: Trobar Books for *Not Be Essence that Cannot Be* (1961); Black Sparrow Press for *Salt & Core* (1968), *The Joe 82 Creation Poems* (1974), and *The Joe Chronicles Part 2* (1979); Kulchur Foundation for *I Am the Babe of Joseph Stalin's Daughter* (1972) and *How Much Paint Does the Painting Need* (1988); New Rivers Press for *Shemuel* (1979); Poetry Around for *Constructs* (1985); and Contact II Publications for *W.C. Fields in French Light* (1986). Parts of *The Joe 82 Creation Poems* were originally published in 1973 by Burning Deck as *Poems from Joe's Garage*; "Anthropologists at a Dinner Party" appeared as a Chax Press book (1985); parts of *W.C. Fields in French Light* appeared as *French Light* (The Press with the Flexible Voice, 1984); and the poems from *Luca: Discourse on Life and Death, Part II* that appear in this volume were originally published as a Backwoods Broadsides Chaplet (1996). The author wishes to express her special thanks to the Rockefeller Foundation for her residency at the Bellagio Study and Conference Center, where she worked on this book.

for George, always

Cover photograph by Mark Weiss; watercolor, "Toscana," by George Economou

CONTENTS

from Luca: Discourse on Life & Death

Part I

Luca: Discourse on Life & Death, begun in 1988, is an on-going meditation on the theme of Mona Lisa and Leonardo.

> The countless images reflected from the countless waves of the sea by solar rays where they strike them produce an immense and continuous splendor over the surface of the sea.
>
> *Leonardo da Vinci*

A Steel Pin

I would like to restrain to circle
myself duration vastness kept at
the edge   masterpiece charred
warped deranged curvature
slanting dissolving   one can sit
wondering in the same position
thinks Mona nailed into space
aerial   sit coldly the young
paysanne
posed sucking her cheeks in she
felt blood saturate

the precise texts record divert
replace the painting

radius there is a woman filling
up geometric signs heavy stones
in combinations mixed confused round
dilation   covered with a white
throw I should not jump the gun
during painful days of sitting
smirking rolling my throat
the whole meaning bursts
throat to jaw drawings numbered
overflowing the atelier
into smoke   burnt offerings

the representation immense
a woman wearing a baffled look
exhaling felt

the shroud   14 feet   3 inches long
3 feet   7 inches wide bears faint

the patient adjusts during painful

11

days of lying

bears faint hidden forms
bears the faint blood-stained image
of a whipped and crucified

woman   Mona intoned but Flora dis-
missed it as forgery

it ought to be Lenny hung on a cross
underpaying the apprentices

slowly I paid a heavy debt

searching the remains of cremations
Flora intoned without end

the white burial cloth stagnates
your transferred fixated

prehistory P

the faint blood-stained slowly
you mesmerize while others dismiss

me as a clever craftswoman
clamping my hand on the nervy brat
always touching things
numbering the codifications coldly

death may be gist essence
evaporization of the motion
sinuous the hairs on the wrists

of Mona who makes a circle faint
thickness calculated combinations
I can no longer do without

blossoms in the mounds of ashes

acid secretions one upon one
another   tickling sensation
a steel pin distilled   the model

moving from the center her fists
clenched reversed pierced anguished
nailed alone   the folds of the dress

trembling in itself dissolution
at the same corner   white wall
above the debris   one cannot
meditate or pray first

I say just do it coldly

aerial cellular into compulsive dots
geometric vibratory at the touch
her eyelid pressed together

ends degenerates infiltrates the
intersections stopping the clicks
heavy stone that this change
and the second described by Mona

watching Lenny snake-dance across
the floor   his face took the space
he coughs the painted plaster flaking
broken collapsed walls
views into perspective
distressed I would create a
sound infection control minimize

disruption serum of intimate paint
you could look to Flora to
remake flexible wound dressings

oneself outside the atelier
the free woman designs evidence

impressions spatial when the arches

spring back the cadaver's teeth
press   a final flowing extend
mitral valve

a final flowing prolapse she said
that the flattened nose the mouth
bone to implant alveolar bone

traumatized this dense gradual
stress & strain tasks of Mona's
posing   all in the self storage
palette equilibrium forms unrolls

but then the skinlike cells of
mathematics contradicts the anxious
breath Lenny shook the lederhosened

nervy brat sitting down & forcing
rolling shoulders Mona saw the tensed
arched foot making circles

but then the boy's abdomen cold
imitating the great Florentine before
I should not jump the gun

repeating increased proceed the last
few years   through an enzyme a great
ocean interchangeable redesigned by
Mona point of prism frozen   holding
her head peasant dress and slanting
smile   posed like a young paysanne
& place the whole meaning in a more
fundamental way

holding her peasant dress it seemed
to her the last few years a compulsive
cycle to force the degree of maneuvers

& place the wads of string her patch
of shimmering scalp burning the outlines
creating multiple brush strokes unlike
a model patient both experimenting
assessing composites myself watching

Mona's eyes smile back secretly after
burning the portrait announcing to
the roving-eyed boy I became a close
friend of Flora that is I paid a
heavy debt but the boy acted so
inhuman at times Mona laughed rolling
her shoulders if I thought that two
fires reduced the sacrifice slung

the heat & noise the escape & pursuit
exhausting beyond suspicion undercutting

Ashes Stuffed into a Niche

like the microscopic species cycles
sliding when the experimenter turns
said Flora searching myself even as

the eyes of the artist needed the
stimuli my crossed cord a strip of
polyethylene plastic the neutral din

felt wads of mucus in the abdominal
section rolling

dysfunction If I thought that two
fires Mona whispered the passage
of throat to jaw leading into the
procedure a mock operation over a
period of years charred beams lying
on the floor of one of the storerooms
undamaged but empty small & hard vessels
left intact Lenny giggled & said that
the floral design broke into dozens
of edges

I should not jump the gun I hook
my neck even further check the
behavior of the brat who watches
the ceiling filled open distance
ruined nearby quivering beneath the
dismembered cadaver the whitish
texture remains of cremations kept
in mind represent life forms come
to grips eager to see more said
Mona her hair plastered to her
head

the friends of Lenny fulfilled

scores of volunteers were adding
cupboards draping a white cloth
over the precipice   on the face
of it the remains of cremations
divided   into two scooped out
ashes stuffed into a niche a
pigeon flying into it by accident

the inner face of the circular wall
numerous vessels of pigment reflected
in the cistern broken & burned with
untouched victuals

the conclusion indicated by its
shape   they had been piled & intentionally
set on fire

a big fire set on purpose a hundred
coins strewn on the floor within a
small radius flat soft little leather
sandals of the child

you startle yourself watching my
film scenario
A nest of grasses
the external flows the celluloid
details   Mona is looking at
a horizontal timber my choice is
to cut away the warped area preserving
the sharp edge descent into limbo
giggled Flora

said she covered with a white

throw those procedures open   distance
I'm painting four people now St. Anne
the brat & Jacomo who came to me on
Magdalen day   1490

the kindness I gave to the despairing

her misdeeds continue giggled Lenny
such wish-phantasies   I hook my neck
even further check the composite
material

said I   it was like snowflakes
my bronchial tubes charred felt dys-
function If I thought that two fires
destroyed that period of Mona's existence

originating in the heart-loneliness
which overtakes most artists of
risk & compulsion chattered Lenny
pursing his lips puckering the facial
nerve wearing a baffled look

"The smile of Gioconda floats upon

her features"

Mona watches the video choosing cellular
hexagons in black stone assessing
fibrous circles screws in the protective
shield

plexiglass on her portrait exposing
Lenny's fibrous memory

heads of women who laugh

Stimuli Graft

evoke Da Vinci blacken the canvas
burn down the stimuli of the laying
on of hands a beginning without end
diagnostic revenge by the merchant's

Florentine wife the space speaks
from defiance the skeletal space
of the atelier hears the burning
spelt out the enigma which resolves

allegorical uterus malformations
of sacrificed lambs a bunch of
despised sheep first there is a
woman the head manipulated

ligament gray in transition lateral
the design fibrous centering a ball
of felt unearthed charred beams
lying blackened within a radius

without beginning the enigma
preserves details the interruptions
into dozens of edges screws Proto-
types together

slowly   I abandon courage said
the disciples posed like young
peasants circling a bonfire

Da Vinci squares his hands

pressing the canvas coldly   his
strained thorax decodes arranges
a presentiment   sketched on a

sheet of paper I look on

water salt sugar protein   artful
I turn this sentence into doubt space
a rim of melancholy

the old master felt a longing
subtle color through your light brown
hayre

rolled her moon-gray shoulders lazily
Lenny painted a pale yellowish red tropical
fruit

my love gallops sang Lenny benignly
draping a white cloth sketching the frontal
view

a depressed & inhibited prostitute
herself available coldly he advised
traces of the useless dissection sighed
Da Vinci slowly you maneuver aspects of
the atelier I came across the pattern
undamaged

a pigeon stuffed into a niche flying
into it by accident slowly I abandon
courage

you manipulate the ligament patiently
slowly you sketch preserving the sharp
edge geometrical my face looks gray
I paid a heavy debt a woman on the loose
her solemn legs under the coarse folds

peasant dress & slanting smile soft flap
of the leather sandals

the turning of my interest from

art to science

you waste the daylight

when he dissected cadavers of horses
& human beings and built flying
apparatus

I comfortably sit before my work
attentive only drifting only the paint
patient slow during days angling

the slow molecular smile

during the long period   the master
occupied himself

Mona Lisa del Gioconda

the sun would not have blazed
nor the trees greened

a curious kind of derangement
and the peculiar glance

the folds of the dress

Flora said she could not bring
herself   visualizing   old age folds
& wrinkles

I say just do it coldly

repeating increase proceed the
first few years through an enzyme
a great ocean cycle sacrificed the

escape & pursuit the last few years

through a prism holding her head

that is I paid a heavy debt my
view burning interchangeable
redesigned   Mona point of prism
frozen holding her head peasant

dress & slanting smile posed like
a young paysanne & place the whole
meaning in a more fundamental way

it seemed to her a compulsive cycle
to force the degree of maneuvers of
the wads of string & place the wads
of string her patch of scalp her
shimmering hair burning the outlines
creating multiple brush strokes

unlike a model patient a patient
model both experimenting assessing
composites myself watching Mona's
eyes smile back secretly after
burning the portrait's left corner

singing to the roving-eyed brat of
Flora   I became a close friend of
Flora that is I paid a heavy debt

because she acted so inhuman at
times laughing rolling her shoulders
slinging the boy on her back
its fetters so that the figure twitched
as revealed in the notebook the type of
the paw   is like a star   animali sighed
Da Vinci a curious kind of derangement
a triangular puzzle Flora tired of bending

& turning her pose making herself available
to the artist a curvature   at his side &

the brat sacrificed dropping his left hand
prefigured the multiple drawings of Mona
that she had sketched during secular week

The simplicity of the frontal view of the
dead Christ taken from the depressed & in-
hibited prostitute   many of the scenes
portrayed related compositional prototypes

Two angles of the floating cysts intrigued
the boy   decreasing his anxiety   & so he
observed Mona concentrated on the hybrid
manifestation descent into limbo giggled
Leonardo as he cut away the warped area
preserving the sharp edge   peasant hands
collapsing dissolving the outer covering
perfectly   do it coldly she advised him
do it cunningly

You shut off your emotions Mona reflected
fluctuating between over-excitement &
bridled imagination   traces of the dissec-
tion useless peasant dress & slanting
smile   bitter earwax in the cleft slowly
the liquid filters through

The work was never cast deterioration badly
damaged   among the world's lost masterpieces

twisting about extremity electric
coagulating

detailing consists of eradicating
involve the disorder the brain of
the Florentine merchant's wife

emerges knowing toward the center
contemplated by   mesmeric

warmth

one from the other she had grasped
everything in a moving inner collapse
of the folds her peasant dress
reflecting in the window glass
oblivious to the noise of the traffic
her refuge close to the stupefaction
of her birth
from the unfoldment running to the
atelier cut by the strange

left corner burnt

offensive mesmeric warmth   to
the atelier I startle myself watching
the drawings numbered the codification
simple done coldly

slowly you maneuver clamping your
hand on the cadaver's femur   the icy
dots

searching an arc of sticks the piles
of debris higher than the geometric
designs   offensive mesmeric
remains of cremations

tendon transplant tilted inserted
active twisting Flora described Mona
held the instrument half-inch secret
elevations

cleansing of the skull degenerative
bitter dug-up   leaving before

that this change and the second just
to the east of the atelier middle

pomegranates vine & fig leaves

a geometrical pattern of ends degenerates
infiltrates the reddish mosaics intersects

black or red bile juice squirts said
Lenny's notes oriented towards searching
the seams of a discarded wallet
the flat piece squeezed she had an

enduring interest in an early source
centrifugal suspicion through collapsed
walls the heaps of heavy stone the tears
in the felt the vomit of the boy the clicks
stop the urine flows   her face took on
a gray scream she writhed & arched her
wrists backwards Flora was looking for
her shoes that the hefty brat had hidden
the rectangular panels black or red
sheer physical revolt Flora found a box
of eyepaint with three stolen golden
chains that her brat had hidden

section of malignant liver abscess
Mona described what was in the bags
sometimes laughing

Da Vinci croons your patch of scalp
shimmering subtle color through your
light brown hayre

a garbage hauler who the authorities
said was unaware of the waste

the red & black cadavers   odor of
silent red clay unspecified number
of syringes 60 loose needles 25 urine
samples 15 blood vials a scalpel blade

5 gold rings   4 petri dishes   3 sperm
samples two black plastic garbage bags
1 trash bin & a partridge in a pear tree

Flora said it's intolerable she put the
lukewarm salt water into the cup of
her hand   she was only here by accident

peasant dress & slanting smile delicately
touching the diagnostic tools she arched
her left nostril imitating Lenny sniffing
a mound of ashes the remains of cremations

she saw snow falling a rim of keloid tissue
she startled herself watching Mona's eyes
smile even as the fetal glance searches
a light source

sickness everywhere   without
secrecy   Flora & Mona

sickness everywhere   but without
mistrust   all the chemicals grouped
reminds Flora & Mona   bears

faint hidden forms   named numbered

the atelier filled with busts statues
funerary altars grouped

but without secrecy   all the chemicals

death may be gist essence

Mona says theorizing what might be
grouped combined coded collected
the substances named accumulated

subtle color through your

light brown hayre

color of mistrust around your floating

smile I am holding

immediacy of the sketch fueling
you

I should not jump the gun maneuvering
this text

onto the shroud   14 feet   3 inches long
3 feet   7 inches wide bears faint

slowly I paid a heavy debt
bears faint hidden forms
grouped heavy stones interchangeable
opened

This work of sfumato active prior
to the arrival shaft stored eggs
this honey & dung that intrigued
the child   but the blood vessels
unearthed benches unplastered the
course of construction Lenny's records
had been written for Lenny alone

semi-circular the brat wandered
into the storerooms the victuals
unburned eaten after the fire in
the atelier the codification simple
geometric patterns the neutral din
intense beyond belief throwing at
once the movements of the model
drawn in the happy periphery turned
inside out you arch your foot

posed like a young paysanne the

enigmatic fetus

the boy down & nail him to a rock
the horizontal timber the maximum
distance pleasing to the boy Flora's
turd spilling fruit juice soaking
through the guiltless lederhosen

Da Vinci's neck hooked over his
work tender he discovers he looks
like a flirtatious peasant girl
moon-gray shoulders Lenny breathing

A hefty toddler runs up to the cadaver
searching for her shoes

gravitation nowhere

an eccentric leap irradiates
looted the atelier before the
fire I came across the pattern of
hexagons saw stuck in the grout
successive geometric signs

ashes from the cremations in heaps

undamaged but empty storerooms
found

found a few pipes the aging master
in a frenzy shook his wrists savagely
which the halo the imaginary personages
filled up the red wine bottles
perfect rectilinear

lazily you touch your tightened
eyelids   the first word of Da Vinci
is pressure epoch Flora said
I startle myself watching your

eyes smile even as the

big eyes of the artist flirt
with the boy   you are about to say
something about suddenness with
which the aspects of definitions
scratch into limbo the immense
ball of felt the vomit

of the boy the hefty brat had
eaten some eyepaint he writhed &
arched his back screaming

this space a light eating the dust stone
splinters geometric noise it belongs to
Mona posed unearthed without end the
contours of the atelier the model neutral

in the space of the atelier closed in the
four thick walls the heat unchained seeping
honey & dung hidden burnt a form filtering
through the wall

soaking through the guiltless lederhosen

guileless objects which to us seem unworthy
of so great a mind allegory natural history
animal fables prophecies of a flirtatious

peasant girl moon-gray shoulders I have
insisted on

slowly I paid a heavy debt my face looks
kind of a gray dove a single line to sketch
and study suddenly it dawns

her slow molecular debt seven days sitting
in the midst

of posters of the caricature shifting her

hip during the long period melon rinds
hidden in my shoes

the nervy brat had shoved   as usual he
squatted down his heart-shaped heinie
swaddled in guiltless lederhosen

behind the opaque tightening
drop therefore   distilled cast obstruct
frozen air volumes   see Mona going from
the center exterior   alone   the folds
of the dress insubstantial   reflection
& effect   of Da Vinci's terror fluidity
in Italy globules blood littleness veins
monstrously enlarged

keloid tissue circumference the dream
separates contracts encloses

running across the floor   white wall above
the utensils   in a corner a heap of mosquito
netting

death may be gist essence

mounds of infectious waste   the sun would
not have blazed nor the trees become green
nor Mona posing   she was here by accident
smiling little eyes posed like a young

paysanne   a sense of isolation silent red
clay   the geometric design faint echoes
puckered   two matched sides   the boy sucking
his cheeks in   the brat writhes & twists
arching his back   his eyes small & hard &
round with disgust   imitating a spider
I said circling the model & the child

distilled cast obstruct   opening & shutting

one's life cooled down   one cannot lift the
eyelids   poison in the debris   I've got
weaving eyes   slowly you startle while

slowly you maneuver clamping your hand
on the cadaver's femur   the icy dots

transparent spots intertwined
she was like a woman who awoke too
early
in the darkness in order not to
be changed

in essence the diversion of
this sentence this version of Mona
& Flora for it was Flora who ought
to have been depicted Lenny intoned

while numbering the codifications
a genuine work of christian art

because it is not the intent of
experts to mislead

I say just do it coldly

searching subjecting the shroud
thin body of fiber manipulated
exposed & opened the skinlike cells
diagnosed

I remember said Lenny when I was
six years old

the hefty toddler runs up to my feet
solidly sits down backwards

his heart-shaped heinie swaddled

in guiltless lederhosen

The Shroud into the Fibers

Mona's brain averts   she turns
the portrait around her eyelids tighten
slow molecular   she was only here

by accident the whole meaning dissolving
bears faint hidden forms

If I tell some traits
reconstruct facts of the inscrutable
portrait   fuel you   as you search
the cremains

your transferred fixated breathing
weaving abnormality

into the fibers of the burial cloth
Flora circles Mona patiently objective
from object to object

grim exposed demolished
mistrusts her notebooks describing
the shroud   14 feet   3 inches long

3 feet 7 inches wide bears faint
hidden forms bears the faint blood-stained

image of a whipped and crucified woman

slowly I paid a heavy debt

slowly I mesmerize while others
dismiss me as a clever copyist just
numbering codifications

how the image on the shroud was

created

all mental disciplines have
been rewritten since something
alien   extent on deviations which

the pagan world deemed natural
riddle of the shroud into the fibers
the shroud bears the faint blood-stained

image of a whipped and crucified woman
a memory of the shimmering hair
through a prism redesigned   interspersed a memory of
Mona burning the shroud
slow molecular   it dawns suddenly
that I cannot bring calm blissfulness
with a blissful smile Lenny's
representation

that I cannot bring the drawings
of the inscrutable Moaning Lisa
to understanding that all these
compositional prototypes of paintings

ransacked

the used image to devour bits of
the edge of the shroud in the end
the author's century   in the middle
of this middle herstory

from the child to the cultural woman

when with chainsaw wearing the shroud
alone says Flora snug but comfortable
fitting work clothes

I put the lukewarm salt water
into the cup of my hand

The Ransacked Atelier

in the space of Mona's atelier
in the end of the century   in the middle
of this pre-history   in the slow molecular
smile

there is a woman deceptively changing
used image to devour deepening the
blood-stained image fueled coldly her
own hand forming geometric hexagons

white mosaic stones dismiss the theory
indicate the evidence that the rumors
of the shroud

preserves details aspects of the atelier

you feel Mona's nausea   rashes   memory
blazed focused the useless invention
defining itself that Flora was fascinated
by Mona's smile

that unfathomable smile always with
lukewarm salt water

near her to gargle with   stress & strain
patient model sitting down & forcing
burning the outlines

views into perspective
fear of infection   the cadavers of
Lenny   she was only here by accident

she put the lukewarm salt water
into the cup of her hand

from Luca: Discourse on Life & Death

Part II

I

attracted the gold silence through which
through which water spreads over
how when groups of the first Spaniards
in America searching

the ore in the night air they destroy
your whitish bones bright red stems mark
mark the corpse gouged with cries of

insane forest land sea-water intones conquests
searching America the groups of Spaniards
destroy your whitish bones now ore
now ore exceeds its value how under their
clothing soaking cell by cell

dark faults nitric acids so that the Spaniards
slash your armpits gouged letters   New Spain
sunlight in the holes   a string of little

a string of little skulls

you take upon your lap blankets there along
the edge plague spreads over you watch
mounted riders folding their arms

tightly twisted around his body raw thongs
her head eyes covered she passes her hands
their attention tracks faults

traces Guatemalan highlands

letters segment one for the crow one
for the cutworm

II   A Circular House

then as she voyages took
took delicate blossoms deviates
from a sixteenth of one

then taking it upon her lap blankets
infected with plague her forearm
tightens spreads over

a cold molecular cloud seeding

sinking through silt ash silt clay

hydrogen helium chalk moves animal
outlines Mona voyages

all over America took delicate blossoms

scattered as leaves sweeten   then
you looked at a circular house
Salia's impudent mouth eating buttons

then she looked at a circular house

saw Salia blowing black dust
he scattered delicate blossoms
cramped his wrist cutting

disgorges dark greens routes

through which water runs spreads over

America

III   Death Cart

invades the body breaks swells scraps of
parchment triples the arms of the cross

ice walls diagonal lines strips of bark
wandering east to west point of pulsation
nearer and nearer gather sap and resin
extract

you lower your wrist plagued by doubt

doubt giving shock and wonder there in
a wood your attention tracks dry black
paint

his jaw falls open the hands and feet
positioned correctly rigid surgical
slashes parchment fused

days of the Maya calendar cross expose
circular sides rifles against the walls
you mistrust

my wrist dark ridge of seam hardness
of surgical scar vivifying

she passes the death cart loaded with
loaded with scraps of metal

Spaniards wearing braided silk belts
Florida through which blood jets
ancient corn plants shadowed upside down
a cooking cauldron

IV   Flora's Labor

struck their faces then remnants of
a cold molecular cloud slowly sand gravel

shaping tendons then she came forth
she came forth dancing disgorged
the ants stealing flowers twisting between
nightfall

Flora sketched skulls grass crevice clumps
head of a mushroom show her menacing
the ants as autumn winter burns veins

burns veins in rock spirals dug each
idol rose nearly as high as the scaffold
Salia idling but drawing a plow

oxen plowing and sowing

lowers his head sinking a paint brush
creating black ants from the dough
from the dough of the corn

I the young cornstalk rose like a

column of blood

she turns her head now she examines
surgical strokes casts off a thousand
cleaved olive pits Flora's labor clouds

twisting outlines then filled clinging
humus disgorges inlines now she
examines Aztec names Mictlan

V   Corn Plants

the horizon falls off in flesh smells
the paste of corn pushing
she drew the body of hair and water
after a few years the Spaniards

crossed origins when the Spaniards
invaded the land your breasts opening
lacterous she voyages all over America

over prairies and forests streams and desert
interwoven raw thongs his speech was
changed burned their speech until
your mouth nearer and nearer

their mouths smell of paste of corn
incantations moving

so that the Spaniards seized the gold
walls drawn in black paint Leo n a rdo
yours are all the tribes your attention
tracks dry black paint

you mistrust lines of letters days of
the Maya calendar how when groups of
the first Spaniards

gold attracted the gold sea-water dark
scrotal sacs

the ore in Yucatan how under corn plants
slashed skin water covers

VI   Red Paint

she faults the drawing became the corpse
along ruin and defeat the legend pulsates
large and small mountains burning

then stripped you saw faults tremble
the bright patterns along the red halves
how when the Spaniards set fire

set fire armed like us the owl and wildcats
nearer and nearer wind made of stone
while she soaks a blanket her wrist cramps

cursing the place fixed and raised his
and raised his hands smeared with red paint
skull and ear veined scrotal sac

how when you are reading a paper about
rivers ravines defeat

spreads over lodges in ear and skull
grains flakes she scattered upon her lap
delicate blossoms through her lips

through her lips black dust seeding

sinking through silt ash silt clay your
attention tracks the first Spaniards
drawn in black paint they stare down

they stare down from white walls
dark-ridged hands and feet dark-ridged
cuts your tongue pulsates lines of letters

lines of letters of penance   blowing
black dust

from Not Be Essence That Cannot Be

1961

Not Be Essence that Cannot Be

ME Agonizes. It it's Brown ME
Which treads, changes, Agonizes. This
Desmodium Venturous. Than the other
(From a tick). Infinite Not Be.
Not Be essence That cannot be escaped. ME
It's brown carnivorous Burrowing Is the like
Beyond Beyond. Illimitable. Outrageous. Known.
Mediocre Mediocre.

Belonged into Sheepshank

Hunger
It is luck too. Hullabaloo Vishnu
Knowledge birds liturgic liverwort dynamite ne-not
Hideous Munt Jak
Barbarous.
Rosy.
Like emblem on the teeth. Two, the best
I pray thee, the nose leaking, the indians, the words
And songs
Nimble-feeted
Enlightened
Be a cold
Thing.
The same time. Tied to no place
Belonged into Sheepshank punjabi delusion
Unreal with no
Thing.
Lived.
Which my Pope. Bent over
Made pregnant ordained bursted the good
Fat foreskin
Sighed.
After entombment
And carpfishes.
Tonkin
Mere not Simon Magus. He was emptied
Before the man and animal mentally
again and again
Between the hole of the mouth
And ass hole.
The base salty.
Some matter. I emit
I hold value and attached butter-fat love

Good selfishness
Burnt clay.
Unclearly christian
For a hump.

Yields

Yields
(Which see)
      Azzas
See which
Picker-tool
Azzas
Wielding
A a growing
Iso-
Lation

Two
That for
Spec-
Ial sperm
Prodigal horse
Spechez
Luminus
Which after
Die. Nine (nin)
Twists made in
Voles   water-
Ing
Juicy

Called Also the Instant

Become limulus sounded minuted Gradual the silent lumps
Worst silent Become limulus Which one which one Which
           Other divi-ded Magni-ficent Made spiry
                 The Maker The kind Judas six of Jul-ius
Receiving O mimicry Zarin pith deigned deigned without
           Worst The foretelling Joseph Smith four feet
In answerable Called also The instant Also the trembling
                 Umbel Tyrr Manx cat And forefoot
     Of And profanation Two Kings shown two spheres reached
     Placed And After Her Of it Tallow Tasmania con-verted
                 Who Who in the fetter That
Is far less Other things The count-ry shrubs and trees

Up Up on the Disorders of the Hairs

The least be be oaklike colorless. Or. Or the
Sweat ducts hither hither Come. Up the nostrils
Tangled incredible. On this genus brass. Yellow.
Being touched hither hither hither hither flat-
Footedness, focus on this genus brass. Yellow.
Yellowish in the fe-male. In the huckleberry.
By the dry withdraw-al.

Get out out the booms, fingers and toes, in the
Arctic friiz of vigor middle finger. That on
The Yucca horse and ass, zinc and male or like
Jove, joyey cheek through the air METHINKS be-
Comes suckling pigs down down on the prickli-
Ness. Up Up on the disorders of the hairs.
Give an eating oil.

Me Hoggish (Hod)

Be-
Loved
Oligocene
Dump
  O
Ducs ME hog
Gish
(Hod)
Knuckling
To two united
Object balls
Psammos sand
Guatemala
    Siccus group
Preside
    (Siccus)
At the bitter
Tupi frondosa
Watermain
Annu Is-sue
Target marquesas
Pig-soil
Uzbek
Rare UZBEG

Me either uva
Of bean door-keeper
Depend ikik
Of axis
  O
Nian
Ab hallowed
Conopodium
Hotch Potch
Terra
Or Alight
On the water
Ab dead
Yaymen
Heil wood
Marked fop
Head fruit
Not lay by with
Splashed
Splashed
7 stomachs
Cuckoo'd
Sun-drying

Lost Tending to Icchen Yicchen

He
Heads
Tiger Eye
Hawse hole. Name enclosed in
Cob nut
Sir Henry in Habana
Cuba. Suckblood
The stems and stalks
Them human heat lighters
Heart land. Health Eaters

Make
Of Georgians
Holy piss of the
Caucasus Formula. Is Atomic
Suborders
In urine and india rubber
Affected in anger. Family gu-blow
The same other number 2 shit
In indigo and kindness
We unnerve not offensive

Culture
Milk
Soil serum
Vatican Councils
Three bones in organik
Enos penos muscle
By intimation
Free mercy wholly
Inmeshed. Loco and chiefly
Lawful

Any genus
Misty mastered.
Go send Mishnayoth
His wrong minus semi
Parasitic American
Pipefish
Sharp point charges
Money shevism pinchcock
Trees spurious flow fluids
Common likened (Hypopitys)
Not significant and genuine

Fertilization
Wife
Fenugreek
Sugarman with water inch
Identical (poison ivy). Jack
It's fictitious
Ithun Ithun. Lost tending to
Icchen Yicchen body of
Eboris Myrna that object
of ginseng saturation
The fruit mulberry yellow-wood

An
Jaloos
No-Ah. Like radical
Kangaroo Hence time
On the balls Jackass
Neck feathers
Reversed forming
Bright blue and
Naught ropes wire
2 minerals
Jad Jad Devotees

Origin
Of Zebedee
Myth. Pal. Serving the
Shape mixture of Japonia
(Native knuckle over the front
Double fist)
Obsequious young latex
Scriptures
Udders
Midst
Soldiers Arms (Mimosa)

That ore
Nor vegetable old
Mine mals sights mass
Phases only old world
And the seeds remote
5 divine offspring ale-wife
(Peace Esox Grinus) Holy place
Spoilt
Peely head developed
Chirp buttercups poagrass
Daringly bountiful

Humble Humble Pinati

1961

Humble Humble Pinati

Seven-teeth spittle, I disarranged prairie-dogs,
Lasted conversion, beheld from

Humble humble pinati, stone letter
Greasy, slug each of me from head to heartstruck
Nerve. Fickle, predaceous, herb herb

What matter if I croak? showing Frog when it
Is with blotch. The other seed plant what slay.
And the teachers Sometimes is written above
Suppose.
Is fall, smartly along Sing Muzhik is not geometry
On your cock, is Scheherazade Queen
Through caution and lemon juice

You you shred wheat, you you fuck sometimes 'nd hide your

Oh what do do, is troubling me, ponderous,
The performance is new, bad, good, is keeping people in stitches
(Then certainly I'm without hope, evening star chromosome

When seriousness is needed, illumination,
Redskin determine, osculate us give us no trouble
With the head. Connection in the ear, O that bears us

Greatly).

Manifesting the love of awfulspring
Comeon, in the conduct, Greetings!
Loose supposition, bizniz under the brave

Bulls, Awful to color red the Chief and give him the bony structure
Vatican City, cellulose Seven Voonder of the

Voorld.

Come on tanze, surcease, knife of diamonds
                    Pinch me, sing out a wild old
                                        Toon.

        Enter the hock, often in the pubic stage, enough to pro
Voke us and Mexico in Space from

                            Tuberculosis, all holy uses holy uses
                Lust, Africa's nipple, a pebble on the sterile moor
        Queer. That he feed, shluck shluck

Is bone the bone and arrow Is bone again I say
                    Fairyman. Down down is hellogram, a blue trademark
                            On the sonoman

        Wif Wif, muffle the sloppy pineapple, on the back of
Elephant, give out a pledge, a dead body cockiness so that poor
                    And poorer pullet chickens
            Make. Build with hard brown wood.

                Come on again! Last this much longer see Stromboli
This is humor which is seen Vision like a hoghead

                    Madre Sicilia pissing on Italy
            Singing and dancing, springing into a province
About to molt herself, whither whither

She goes, piggy piggy she is no stern girl she like to dance
                    She is not bleached, not worn-out and praying
                            She is called Ready Ready

                    Come Tomcat.

        Arrest. They like to meet again, to bind bread to smoke
                Meat (is not a rubber jaw) A weakling
                        With a tick tick
Thumb-sized forebear, ancestor, come on squeeze her colorless ear.

Pull the tooth, a bed of roses for the tooth
Dome dome uncle sam Artery arm do not pipe down. Is designating
A buttock for the velvet cushion, keep for the flesh, man

Is a baby, spilth his little gut,
Mortify, spout his vitamin, little lamb-tongue
Suppose suppose we did. The goat prick would peeper out

Smally.

Five parts red berries usually
It goes pentecostal, yield, again I say
See the strange Voorld, converse, bring

A insect into the Mass, see if it like cane sugar and loves swollen

Supremely good sculpture. Then we can tell
On it.

Charger, father, throughout the holy day, through mortar
The throat, her teachings
Betray me.

Goon. They stole a nat-ive, in the mood they pulled
His pants off him give him sweet potato

Tending to go back, endurance,
Tame my criminal, kiss a jackdaw. Virgo, virgo
Prickle his part, destroy

Is the shalt not spicule known of news or a damn
Weaker growth? False false is the new thought
A game miser, we play

Back, back, four times timed by four, the silky symbol
I plunk it down, kill it for food
Watch.

from Four Young Lady Poets

1962

Penobscot Bird

tending palpa
bility, outer tingling season
wading bird, last year's, upright and red
rude up and down, against calf of the leg. super
stitious Only showing organism
and the raised filthy head,
or back, pepped into a seed, his illusion
shot, folded into shit, seeking between soft food and
a light and a lilac.
it is inherited of the Penobscot bird.
and on the end bean meal
fluke, rigid like a piping teacher-bird, again
jingling, cultivated joint-worm, white chattering, pantingly,
excessing sex, preening
for inch and a half red larvae.

from Elga's Incantation

1962

from Elga's Incantation

for Ronald Bladen

YES GOD PUT A BODY ON COME ON BACK & RISE WHILE
I'M IN THE FLAESH LIKE YOU YES & IT MUSH BE THAT'S
RIGHT MUST BE WRITTIN OF THE LAW MOSES MUST BE
FULFILLED MUZIC & DAVID WAS A O FOOL & SLOW OF
HEART & GOD WANTED THINGS DONE & THEY FELL DOWN
& HE ROSE LIKE A PROVERB SO NOBODY PLAYS MUZIC IN
AMOS' HOUSE. HYPOCRITES DON'T WANT TO SING THEY
MAKE NOT NO SONG YES YES YOUR IMAGE IS YOURSELF
GOD DIDN'T WAT? WANT THEM TO SING YES & THEY EAT
UP THE CALF IN THE STALL THAT WAS WRITTIN IN THE LAW
OF MOSES UMHUM YES THAT'S RIGHT DONE PREACHED &
PRACTISED ALRIGHT BEND OVER & RECEIVE GRANDMA'S
THUS GRANDMA CHECK UP ON ME GO THIS WAY NOT THE
OTHER WAY THE OTHER WAY IS HELL FROM & ME GET ME
CLEAR NOW I'M BACKED UP BY THE ON THEE TRUE
CHURCH BEGAN AT JERUSALEM NOWHERE CUN A WOMAN
BE A DEACON & YOU CANNOT MARRY WHILE THE OTHER
SPOUSE LIVES BECUZ OMMISSION OF SINS IN THE NAME
OF JESUS NOT FATHER SON OR HOLY GHOST IN THE NAME
OF JESUS CHRIST BEGINNING IN JERUSALEM FOR ALL
NATIONS UH HUH YOU'RE MY WITNESSES I'M GONNA
SEND SOMETHING ON YOU I'M GONNA SEND THE HOLY
GHOST ON YOU & JUDEA & SAMARIA EVERYTHING'S
GONNA SPRUNG UP YOU HEAR THAT? YOU GOTTA FOL-
LOW THE APOSTLES TO HITTING OF THE END OF THE EARTH
DON'T GO AWAY FROM JERUSALEM OBEY NOBODY'S
GONNA HAVE AN EXCUSE? WHO? NOBODY NOBODY WILL
GET AWAY AMEN. PETER & JAMES & JOHN & ANDREW &
THOMAS ARE FOLLOWING ME & SUPPLICATION WITH THE
WOMEN & MARY THE MOTHER OF JESUS & MAARY &
MAARY THE MOTHER OF JESUS MAARY THAT MEANS
EVERY WOMAN IN THE WORLD ACCORDING TO THE
HOLY GHOST COME & GET IT ARE YOU LISTENING WO-
MEN? WITH THE WOMEN & MARY THE MOTHER OF JESUS

MISTER! THAT MEANS EVERY MAN IN THE WORLD WHA?
HAPPENED COME & GET THE HOLY GHOST BOTH LORD &
CHRIST WHAT? HAPPENED THEY WERE PRICKED IN THEIR
HEARTS IN WHAT NAME? IN THE NAME OF JESUS CHRIST
HOW DO YOU KNOW HE WAS CALLING? EVERYBODY
BAPTISE YOURSELVES THIS COMING MONDAY MORNING
EVERYBODY IS WELCOME REGARDLESS OF HIS RACE.

* * *

Ziz jumbo mammal piles bugs EVERLASTING worse than in
the beginning of a marigold she SO took to tremblings and
whinnies wanting redemption wresting the FALSE right, sin
wrong, where seasons move into a ball do not sufficiently
move with that roosting god; to get the suckling she-wolf with
the snout in the month of May or Ju-ly get her while she sleeps
or stands; and bes fearful lest the lip becomes jet-black during
life as in death; result to be fed while living keeping the cycle,
over and over the earthen pot the meat is jerked like the wing
of a crane, choicest of postures. Holy muteness. The roll of
the kidnapper—killing the kid but he gets rocked as he hangs.
& in the kidney is a sickness—young men don't fall it's in my
urethra—with the rope I hold I keep you from the gloam, give
pearls & cowpeas & apples to you—used not to be nervous so
much. We were malicious together and unWorthy we were
shameful in north america 499 persons to choose from & we
choosed each other jogged our hearts up with open eyes on
each other. It's a fit time to suffer in all our four limbs or even
one foot. It's a messo. We were not white with each other we
breathed like bell jars our heads stuck out from like a swamp.
Till we got loosed.

* * *

O MI DARLING I'M GETTING DEAF O MI DARLING I'M GET-
TING DEAF O MI DARLING I'M GETTING DEAF O MI
THARLING I'M GETHING DEAFTH O MI THARLING I'M
GETHING DEAFTH O MI DARLING THARLING YOU A TWO-
BIT STARTHLING THO I'M GETHING DEAFTH O MI DAR-

LING I'M GETTING DEAF O MI DARLING I'M GETTING DEAF
O MI THARLING DARLING YOU A TWO-BIT STARLING SO
I'M GETTING DEAF I'M GETTING DEAF MI DARLING I'M GET-
TING DEAF O I'M GETTING DEAF & DEAFER THAN YOU O
MI DARLING THARLING LISTHEN TO ME O LISTEN WHILE
I BECOME THE DEAFEST O MI DARLING YOU'RE GETTING
TO BE THE DEAREST TO ME WHAT DEPTH IT IS TO GET DEAF
YOU HEAR O MI THARLING MI THARLING MI THARLING
O MI DARLING SO OO O O SO O O MI DARLING When in
the half part she caused him to go lower, making thus a natu-
ral body of course, moving on him loudly with trickery, a
philo-sophical wench and dirty bitch on a bicycle (HIM)
becoming his bread (her) her muscles rioting at the end of the
dinner O MI DARLING I'M GETTING DUMB O MI DARLING
I'M GETTING DUMB TELL ME ABOUT THE FRANKISH EM-
PIRE AND THE BUSH CRANBERRY AND THE DITHER OF AN-
CIENT BATTLES AND WHO ENDOWED ME WITH BEAUTY
AND WHY I'M WISE AS A PENNY & WEIGH SO MANY
POUNDS. WHO IS HUMMING IN THIS BURG? WHAT IS THE
NAME OF THIS BURG? HOW MANY PEOPLE LIVING IN THIS
BURG? HOW MANY ARE UNNATURAL IN THIS BURG? O MI
DAR-LING I'M DUMB O MI DARLING I'M DUMB I'M SO
DUMB MI DARLING TELL ME HOW So she got a slight shake
indeed the truth which isn't puzzling indeed indeed she might
have become a suicide that's a numbing thought though though
1 of every 3 young used to die though probably in the days
when men fought in their nakedness the first poke would kill
them though but what excitement! What excitement what
cockeyed excitement think of the young men lying like ripen-
ing cheese in lands not their own mouths near each other
saying gush to the god of war gush gush we are not so good
for marrying now what woman would have acquaintance with
us now now that we're shrinking in death now that our heads
are concave and our blood and sperm become just mixed color.
What is this nasty talk? LAMB-OF-GOD DISGRACEFUL ELGA
SAYS SHE IS AS LOVELY AS A BUTTER-AND-EGGS FLOWER
LAMB-OF-GOD PUT ELGA'S NAME IN THE DOOMSDAY BOOK
PUNISH HER MAKE HER FEEL A BIG LOSS MAKE HER LITTLE
EYES BE PUT OUT SHE DAST NOT KNOW NOTHING BUT

BAD KNOWLEDGE GET-HER-THE-FUCK-OUT-OF-HERE BA
BA BABUP A BUPADUP BUPPA BUPPA DUP DUP O MI DAR-
LING I'M GETTING BLIND O MI DARLING I'M GET-TING
BLIND O MI DARLING I'M GETTING BLIND O MI DARLING
I'M GETTING BLIND O MI DARLING I'M GETTING TO BE
FULL OF DOUBT BLIND WIPING OUT THE WISDOM OF SOL
WIPING OUT OF MY EYES DINAH'S AMERICA SO I SHOULD
BE BLIND WHOLLY

* * *

Hearken that I'll not be free from harm or unscrupulousness;
that there will be those who will want sand in my mouth &
all my other open parts. So that now and then I will not speak.
They will hinder me. & obscure me. so Something grinds at
me like the flesh grinds away from the bone in the work of
butchery, something so affects and grinds at me like in that
nasty work, making my thoughts imperfect, aggravating my
wish to stick the pigs so they'll die & stink finally. & I'll not
be tyrannized anymore after they let go like pus from a sore
something so ugly. So exists it & bes everywhere. So you watch
my feelings.

* * *

ONE WAS ONLY IN B.C. SAID BLOW HEALTH! SAID MARY
IN HIGH SPIRITS ONE THING! I LOVE TOYNBEE WOULD HE
BECOME A PAUPER & FORGET THE EASY MONEY OF WRIT-
ING BOOKS & WAITING FOR THE NEXT FREEZE & EXPLAIN-
ING AWAY EUGENIE'S TROUBLES BECAUSE OF LOUIS

THE WILL OF GOD AND LIKEWISE ARMIES
BECAME DIVIDED THUS THEY USED IT THE
ARMIES VERY GOOD PRONOUNCED AR-
MEEYS AND WAITED FOR JESUS LIKE A LEG-
O-LAMB & THEN THE EXECUTION WAS
MANY PLACES AND IN BO-HE-MIA AND

WRATH WAXED HOT ON THE LEFT AND
RIGHT AND THERE WAS A RIFT IN THE
WEST & TOYNBEE KNEW BEST & WHY
EVEN OF WARS COLD REASONS EVEN OF
THE STRUGGLE OVER GOODS BUT IT'S HIS
SCHEME THESE COMING JUNE DAYS.
THAT HE WILL BE DEGRADED IN ITALY IS A GOOD & WILD
NOTION FOR HIS THINKING IS IMPERFECT & ONLY IF HE
WERE FLEET OF FOOT MIGHT HE NOT MAKE A FINAL
OUTCRY IN OLD TESTAMENT ANGUISH LIKE WHAT JUST
PASSED

THE END OF HISTORY.

NO.

CERTAIN FOODS
(THESE LETTERS SPELL: C E R T A I N   F O O D S)

certain   foods

1. c a r r o t s
2. e g g s
3. r a b b i t s
4. t u r n i p s
5. a p p l e s
6. i n t e s t i n e
7. n o u g a t
8. f l o w e r
9. o r a n g e s
10. o l i v e s
11. d a t e s
12. s a l t   (Is salt food or is used just to season
                     food?) Then why have certain (note the
                     word certain) animals gone over land
                     and dale to lick salt from a salt lick? If
                     it were not food?)
Look in the romances you'll find salt mentioned at least once.

Give yourself a scratch test and bleed and taste 'twill be like salt.

WITH A BIG SCREAM A NEW RACE WILL EMERGE FROM OUT OF UNSCRAWLY THIGHS THE BONES WILL BE BIG AND THE HEADS LONG AND THIN O FOR THAT DAY WE WAIT AND WE WILL HAVE ALL WOKENED AT THE SAME TIME

***

THE DAY OF JACK

Today in the day of Jack, it's a base day, a semicircle of false witnesses meet to talk of the African Stork. After the Jizo Psalm is sung the chief VitaminC tells his twelve that he will go up to the mountain and again argue the anybody up in the sky, to the death.

Suppose out I came
to destroy one foot
against the other
& one eye
made to fall in urine & excrement
to bring about
a gyp
& no answer

I think that I'll run amok
& not do a favor
the stingy mewing job
of living
called the Gyp

And that was JOR'S SONG OR JACK'S the one voice unequal 3 times 12 fellows or 36 stuffed in a barrel. UNRAISE THE DEAD YOU FUCK-OFF. But JOR continued to sing.
In haste indeed
did the people on the west side

of Greece become wild & silly children
they plaited the hairs on their heads & sang arias
Then I, JOR, came along
& made them marry civilly
so that they stopped
fornicating like crabs stopped
being bone-black in the sun

Like the busybody he was JOR tossed the ball & made the twelve
swallow it & the soap & glass & his Zoroastrianism & the
mastery of business science. And sang like a bobolink again

I don't degrade
wholly the hole of my wife
my yellow red purple wife
I never played a practical joke
or kissed any pig's poke

And this JOR had a theory of poetry.

if in the fixture
maybe the gas one, like the features
of a face or the rectal tract
there is a movement

for a development in the mongolian language
a pulling apart of beds for babies

AHAA THE FUFKIN SKOOL-BOY WON'T STOP I SAY STOP
JOR BEFOR HE STOPS US! YAY HE'S LIKE A CANCER AT-
TACKING ONE OF THE THREE TRINITIES THEN HE'LL GET
THE OTHER TWO! I SAY GET A PISTOL & FEND FOR YOUR-
SELF HE'S TRYING TO ALTER NATURE DO YOU NOT FORE-
SEE THE DANGER OF JOR I'M LOATH TO LET HIM LIVE EFFEN
HE KEEPS IT UP ALL HE REALLY LOVES IS A REVOLVING TRAY
OF FOOD O GAD I NEED WATER HE'S SUCH A FRAUD! AND
HE'S SMACKING HIS LIPS THINKING OF MY ANKLE-

JOINTS GAD HE'S ANOTHER FAT CAT LIKE OLD EZ TALKS ABOUT!

And Elga was in terror as a milch cow turned purple. All in her head was three words mum mum mum. ABC DE ABCED she said trying to keep pure & heavens her nervous system it grouped around in her belly like the little dipper in the sky, she chewed her hair in the nightmare of JOR while a winged cockroach said the gospel in rote & a hippopotamus sucked an iceberg & a hunk of moss tried to make love to her & all in an hour this all flowed past like the development of a frog but 'twas really 6 days & after she was a dweller on earth & thought of God's artful spirit like in old Babylon He the eternal one tore it apart, naughty Babylon & those that were there were doomed to terror Aye that's what happens to those who are hostile. Now light in the southeast was Nero's cunning too & see what happened to him, the walls were pulled down by fire & Nero did not have a chance to ponder while he burned. Whole throngs of Angels of the race of Adam ate the apples of joy while Nero suffered. IN THE HOPE OF THEE IN THE HOPE OF THEE BANISH FROM ME THE PAIN THE KNIFE THE POMP OF THE WOUND THE GRIM TORMENTS THAT CRY LIKE A CUCKOO MY AFFLICTION PROMPT UP MY SPIRIT TO HEAVENLY HARMONY AT DAYBREAK & EVENIN AT DEAREST & SWEETEST TIME SAVE ME FROM RAGING & FURY

***

from Salt & Core

1968

The Power of Love
He Wants Shih
(Everything)

First, I put my
hands on her—shou meng haou!
I'll show you.
I make my arms hard
against her softness—
she sighs
her love for me
is my weapon
the feeling ceases
in me
& her feelings
increase
her skin under
my fingers feels
like blood
not yet dry
a star on fire!
& I feel wrath in me
& melancholy   &
ice against my teeth & also
      a tiny joy.

If I said to her what
was inside me
the words would be   I will punch you
to pulpwood!
The sounds I would make
would be the screams of a
vulture against
her throat.
Her mouth & legs   are open
but my mind is working.
It's heaven's will, shua hsi!
In my mind I smear the mucus

from my nose on her breasts
& drop ants into her two mouths
I fill up all her orifices—
I'm very generous
& she calls me the divinity
of mountains & streams &
I think of how it would be
to piss on her! She calls
herself happy & blessed &
how she feels privileged
to love me & protect me
so that I will never feel
lonely or frightened again!
I'm thinking how it
would be to throw her
into a pig-trough—
the pig slop squashing
under her buttocks &
her breasts jiggling
like rabbits!
I made her brim over
like a dark pool
with my tricks—my magic!
She kept her eyes always always
on my belly, it seemed to me
as if she expected nightingales
to fly out of my belly!
& I told her stories!
Stories that I felt she must
hear!
     I
       wandered
             along
      with her
           in her mind
        at my own sweet will!
    While
        I wandered with her
        I minced her

into
         meatballs!
I am a magician!
            & an acrobat!
& that is enough for me!
      She is a
          mouse
       with its
       intestines
           hanging
             out
I think she wants
          to seize me
     & grab
          & scratch
    & tickle me
inside my head is an ax
        & I cut off her head!

What is that?
      the pigeons?

Where Cosh and Tanh Flow

as it must of course be
(the gray gas)
we are dependent
on that condition
where air water and oil
where cosh and tanh flow
in a droplet
it is mixed homogeneously
(this is the life one
is interested in)
by conviction
we hold the rails down
Yet Means The Great Thickness
Earth

in a steady state reaches
the temperature of metal
Yet Means The Great Thickness
Earth
as it must of course be
the gray gas
we are dependent
on that condition
where air water and oil
where cosh and tanh flow
in a droplet
it is mixed homogeneously
this is the life one is
interested in
       by
        conviction
    we hold
        the rails
     down

in a
     steady state
  we reach
    temperatures
of metal
   our
     skulls
        heat up

from I Am the Babe of Joseph Stalin's
Daughter   1972

Dedication

DIN

who am i floating
                    above cows
YAHOEL AM I
                    whiter than   white
            animal skins   unblemished
                                lambs. my blood
so red & light salty
                    Isaac Resnikoff
            the pious scribe
                            studies my .word.
        it is as if sacred white scrolls
        encase my holy legs   Rising I Rise

            over this peculiar

                    continent
                            I float
            above cities   singing glory glory glory
I am living prayer &
                    THEY give me their
            .love.
                    I Am That I Am
            DIVINE STERNNESS
                        *

            J U D G M E N T
        DIN

The Voluminous Agony of Karl Marx

Izzy sells out the worker's party!
I'm the prophet! The dreamer!
The mystic! The plumber! The plumber
of fat sweet sweet revolution!
I love my family! I want them to laugh!
I have all the perception & intelligence
to write the book on economics!
I will sit—I will sit on my boils
in the British Museum & write on economics!
I am the coming judgment! Economics!
My veins are religious with economics!
Who is Karl Marx! I am Karl Marx!
I hate the passage of time without revolution!
I want to cheat the day & the night!
Yahweh! Yahweh! I am a fish sticking out
of the hand of God! I would like a new
gold watch for Christmas! Yahweh! Yahweh!
I have pain! I have pain! I am abused by
historical forces! Revolution which is past
& revolution which is to come! Yahweh!
Let me play Karl Marx! Let me play a workman!
I have got big calluses! Boils! Calluses! Boils!
Calluses! Yahweh! I do a jig for thee!
I have a big izzy in my pants—let me hang
it out for thee! Give me back my foreskin,
Yahweh! I have heard of the Socialist Party!
I've never heard of the Socialist Party!
Look in my eyes! Do you see politics in my eyes!
Or economics! Rage! Rage & pain! Yahweh! Yahweh!
You gave me boils! A family to support.
Six mouths to fill up with groats & milk!
Hate is stuffed into me with my Jewish mother's
milk! I want to write the philosophy that will
burn down all other philosophies! I want to

kill all those who see ideas! Not economy!
Yahweh! Yahweh! Am I right! Yahweh! Yahweh!
Give me the weapon! Give me the weapon that
will kill! Give me the force! Give me the force!
Give me the force to set my teeth on edge &
eat fire! Please! Please let me be able
to sit down like a man should—without pain!
Please let me be able to write the book! Please
take away the filthy boils! Yahweh! Yahweh!
You piss-stink filthy Babylonisch bastard
are you powerless to heal!

The Queen of Greece

The Queen of greece stuck out her big purplish toe (Elga has started a whispering campaign in this place of the history) it had hit the night before or rather it had been pressed like a fat rude grape into the eye of a humble slave. The eye of the slave was brown and the Queen's a brilliant green (her eye) like the c   ian could cast peace like hunks of bread on the waters.

    o   g

    l   e   what an effect

    dA

& the Queen was not hated but loved. Her femur bones were those of a Viking. Strong. East & West North & South of Greece wished for femur bones like the Queen's for their own little infant lads & lasses. Healthy healthvthyhealthye chanted & droned the priests in all the tiny churches in the mother-blood land. A babe was plumpked thiinn into the baptismal slush a babe was plumpked faatt into the oily green water. Plosh plosh went tiny babes smiled tiny eyes into the thick corneas of the plumpker-priest his razor-sharp little-finger-nail leaving a purplish little island on the belly. The-babe-was-wrapped-all-in-white-linen like a fair cowboy in an american song plumpk went the first consecrated turd against the bosom of its mother.

& the Queen of greeccc smiled & said that it was good. It was she who & only she who could split apart the sweetness & light from the dark. You ask why not the slave be mad at the Queen for the above eye injury? Ask then why not a mother be mad at her birth pain after the little child lies in her arms. Never Never are we angered by the marvelous. All over greece you could hear she has a marvelous shape, he has a marvelous shape, they have a marvelous shape. From tailor-shop to tailor-shop as the fitters finger hooked crotches into shape, you would hear the proud voices rise & rise with admiration, WHAT A MARVELOUS SHAPE. The Queen had set the standard with her maddening & insulting beauty german wreaking wonderfully sweet tyranny like blue cornflowers blue

cornflowers on her subjects & the Queen WAS a German though
she spoke greek. For four hundred years the Turks ruled the greeks
& the greeks could never forgive them for that though the blood
of both hard-twisted into each other like passionate grimaces. So
to get even they chose a German woman for their Queen for who
next to a Turk is as cruel as a German
        wound
           twist
              blow
                  iron
                      suck
                          succulence
of beauty reassemble the people
                     stretch
                         them   into
wondrous bigness
            smash us fair Dorians
                          make us fertile sludge
so that we might at least
              make rich the tired old
                          la
                          n
                         d
high high class make us high class people say we are dark we are
not dark
        ICH VILL BRAK YOUR AHM

A large statuette of a nude girl, from Berœa in Macedonia and now
in Munich, has relatively severe forms and must still date from the
fifth century. On the other hand, the so-called Pourtales Aphrodite
in London and the Haviland Aphrodite in New York named after
their former owners illustrate the Praxitelean style in its full de-
velopment. Here too the change from fifth-century monumental-
ity to fourth-century grace is clearly shown.

      VE TEK AVAY YOUR EMACIATED YOUTHS 'ND GIF
                                YOU
                       POSEIDON!
     VE STUFF 'M INTO A SCHLUMBERING CRATER!

IGLE OF ZEUS CARRIES OVV YOUNG GANYMEDE!

The small-faced be-wigged 40ish man whose licorice eyes point
out of the mosaic byzantine-style says happily that the Anglo-
Saxons settled America. His own lips are like brown-glaze very
eastern mediterranean.

I VILL NOT EFEN POOT YOU INTO ZEUS'S IGLE SOUP!

Portraits of the Queen are all over Athens they make her eyes even
lighter than they actually are her nose slants off into the mists of
the north her laughing luscious mouth makes the people calm &
clean
feeling

Nevertheless, as Egyptian sheets have survived, it is likely that
they were known to the Greeks also, even if they were not in
common use... To judge by the many representations of couches
on Greek vases, a bed was not made up as nowadays, with sheets
& covers tucked in. Instead the covers are merely laid on top of
the bed. Mattresses, however, were substantial.

The Queen tapped the golden knob with her porcelain finger &
the green-blue mediterranean sea flushed her normal turds away.
She bragged once to her servant that she had never been consti-
pated. Her breath healthy-sweet testified to that.

```
            greek sailors fantastic humans
                    suck each other
                            off
                 they shoulder MONSTROUS
                            burdens
                 black eyes scrape the
                            skys
          a                    sperm makes
   rorschach p  t  erns
             t
                    on the    av'ns
                        he
```

90

MYTHOLOGICAL SCENES
are picked out from
between the teeth
like strings of lamb
stringbeans & oyl
fuck you turk
turk you fuck
I fuck you in your baklava
I spit in your CASHEW
I make you suck off my
HELMET
I make you scale my fish
shine my olyve oyl
eat my chinese cookie
may you have a bung hole
W I D E as a Thracian jug   may your ass
slope
so
low
dow
off   n
that your buggerer flys
MAY YOU NEVER HAVE THE PLEASURE OF COMPARING YOUR
6 inch elbow
WITH A TURK'S
MAY A TURK SPIT IN YOUR FATHER
THE PRIEST'S EYE
MAY AN IMAM fart
in
your
eye

MAY HE WHACK THE KORAN OVER YOUR
MOTHER*S
H
E A
RT

may your own kind never invite you to
a party

                    may you dance the circle dance
          with pure turks
                    may they flip
                              their white snotrags
                    in your greasy
                              face
          while they whirl their dance
                    around
                    you
                    may you do the 8th & 9th
          EASTER PRAYER
                    UNDER THE EYE OF A
                    TURK-PRIEST
                              & MAY YOU NEVER
                              KNOW
                              IT
          UNTIL HE'S ALREADY PRAYED
                    FOR
                              YOUR
                              DE
                                   AD
                              SOUL

                    ...such was the expressive
sort of talk the greek sailor did, occupied himself with...

Meanwhile, back in the palace at Corfu the Queen slung her fabu-
lous breasts into the most expensive fabric in the world which I
know not what its name is called...better than silk though come
all the way from Paris or Cairo...
                    & may all your joys
          be little turks   may all your business
                    transactions be with cheating
                              turks
                    may your own mother turn turk
                              on
                              you
          & MAY THE QUEEN NOT LIFT A FINGER TO SAVE
                              YOU

& the Queen never would. Why should she? Would you?

Wouldn't you like to sleep on silk sheets like Madame Chiang Kai-shek? Wouldn't you like to donate money to Wellesley College, so fancy? Wouldn't you like to have your picture on the front & back of a diamond mirror? Wouldn't you like to be the picture of beauty on a bas-relief with curly-golden-hair? Wouldn't you like to sit on a horse dragging somebody by the hair, a slave perhaps? WHAT ARE YOU GOING TO DO THOUGH WHEN PEOPLE ASK YOU & YOUR BROTHER TO PLAY the-two-dogs-in-the-street? what are you going to do when people call you a fat beast & not a thin warrior what are you going to do when your life-like-pose looks dead & smelly? what are you going to do when you look down at your legs & see two busted pieces of sausage instead of long-white-limbs? what are you going to do when your one good eye turns inward like ringworm under your one-inch-piece-of-skin that's left of your poor body? what are you going to do when the tears that press out of your eyes are like little blobs of grease & they slip down your zatch making everything you say sound as sensible as a turtle? what are you going to do when the only smile that slides on your face is when some enemy of yours has died & that's every 2nd minute of your life

...the whole gesture of the sailor is that of attack...
        the gesture of everybody
                who wants
        a lotus instead of an ear
              or a pail of rain
                    w
                      a
                  ter
        instead of a bladder

John Wayne who is loved over the entire eastern mediterranean except in Jordan & that*s because they know he's a jew, said

      "WE'RE BEING STABBED IN THE BACK & SOLD
                DOWN THE RIVER
     BY the orthodoxy of the north

                    the blond nation
            the fat russkies
                    the lumpy ukrainians
            the gooky georgians
                                etc
                                    etc"

The final polishing was done with smooth stones & a lubricant...
The Queen had her pubis shaved & an expensive croatian lubri-
cant rubbed on her prickling skin. "Ich habe genug," she smiled
up at the eunuch*s eyes. Her smile was archaic, her cunt modern
& curved so fleshly, her feet squared, the toes like pinkish stone
dipped in & out like tongues. The Queen of Greece commanded
that the lithe eunuch ('twas no crime to be a eunuch in byzantium)
put on a velvet dildo & satisfy her till she quaked from skull to
heels...

                    the
                        xciting
                        storys
                            yu've heard
                about Catherine the Great
                                    are totally false
she never died on a bull...
                    the Queen of Greece commanded the
                eunuch to be beautiful
                                & tell the story of a part
of the history & he said:
                        7 times was the first sentence said
& he said:
                arabs confront byzantium
                arabs confront byzantium
                arabs confront byzantium
                arabs confront byzantium
                arabs confront byzantium
                arabs confront byzantium
                arabs confront byzantium

                        Persia,

94

                           take over
persian's system of hereditary rulers versus turk's more
   democratic
                  Shiites & Sunnis
                           they conflict
the fucking Seljuks are on the move in 1000 a.d.
                                   advance into the
            Arabian Empire
The Queen*s breasts were sucked
                           Turks turn west toward
            A N A T O L I A

confront byzantium defeat byzantium devastate byzantium
              & then alas the nomadic conditions, livestock
   everything on the decline
                     & guess what
                           Turks accept Islam
in the eleventh century
              & the Ottomans come!
                           in the thirteenth
                           century the Mongols
                           invade
            R U S S I A

50,000 families settle in Anatolia & the Ottomans are ruled by the
Seljuks. (the eunuch quickened the tale) Osmanlis absorbed greeks,
byzantine citizens, the 4th crusade & Latin invasion destroys the
byzantine empire arab missionaries instruct osmanlis to accept
conversion greeks are absorbed into the system architecture chiefly
arabic, persian byzantine & the turks innovate the minaret arab &
byzantine two great civilizations but arab civilization destroyed
by the mongols much intercourse in the 13th & 14th century be-
tween turks & greeks turks absorb more & more greeks islam
appealed to them

                     & the Queen smiled
         at her
               eunuch
                  (no shame)

                           95

"I absorb you too," said she.

                            "Do you like my big garden?

                flowers, cauliflowers, parsley, oregano

                      all that growth

                  makes your nose twitch

                Stand up next to the golden broc

                                  a

                                      ded

                  gown

                        near the wall

       with the tapestry of Christ

                  ha   ng

                  ngi

                        & stroke your dildo

      that I may see it & delight in that you have

                  no

                    shame

      in front of me The Queen"

(meanwhile Elga fled hither thither from the brightness & the
bigness with joy) tall broken rocks under her hands decimation of
wickedness beating about bushes squawking of trumpets mighty
cheers Lord Jesu Christ what a wonder on this spot where a eu-
nuch makes love to a Queen

                      So

                    much

                      do

                        I

                          love

                              thee

these breasts
bare to thee
thee man of men
through the throes of
what niceties

          befall thee

                I am smitten

            with love

                I wish thee health

liquor to drink
                all goodwill
          life with no shame
                          no deadliness
          no slavery
     silk brocade to kiss
                     no chaos
          sweet smoke
                     Holy Wisdom
     piety
          Z O E

I Am Deebler Woman

I

If I had $235
I'd go off
to Barbados

Are you in sight
of that amt of money

tell me quick-ly
before I get mad &
cut your nose off.

I work for you for 3 hours &
charge you $15.50 cents
but I'm an old Jamaican

grandmother

with 18 grandchildren
every one of them puts

BIG CURSES

on your hd.

II

first I eat up 3 little ham-
burgers/ are you
sure they not have a bit
of pork in
them?
Do you have children?
My daughter has 8
her first husband is evil.
I eat some crackers
now. Mum.

I've known a lot of men with
steam in their wongs
ha-ha that's a West Indian

figure of speech.
Dr. Kildare is my nephew the english
marry with Black
folks.
My 3rd husband died
of the
CLIMAX.

III

I think that jesus was a Devil
                Woman who liked squash
        & tomatoes.
                        And do you know
    that in the islands we had honey-bees.
                I think that in new
        york they put water in the stuff.

One time a little baby died
        & the mother ate honey
                after.
                        A big pot. I hope
                it crash down on her foot.

        sometimes sand in the fingers
                feels good
            you put your mouth
                            on it   it feels
                    like sugar

        it MUCH BETTER than white sugar.

IV

I would have treated
president Kennedy
good.   I would make him feel his religion
more the catholic
faith is free plane fare to
god.

I keep a little something sweet
chocolate or a bit of
cake
around in my clothes or
bags
life is killing me
sometimes
I know the Jews don't eat
pork nayther.
jesus was a man
who was no pig
he would not
eat the meat from pigs.
A Jamaican woman
should do what jesus does.

V

the Jacqueline woman
president Kennedy's woman
is a hot shit woman
she has the most
beautiful soul   her eyes look
very evil
like my daughter's husband
the Roman Catholics
have stomachs full of the
religious passion.
I still believe it
nobody can take
god's place/ no matter what
political fools say
I like hard/
very dark brd
with the butter from
the indian peanut
it takes away
the sickness
that this island puts
in your body.
I am a GOD WOMAN
would you let me buy yr earrings?
I would thrill
when you fall dead at my
foot.

from The Joe 82 Creation Poems

1974

Wild-Woman & the Second Moment of Science

                        & the Naked direction   the
            shape
            Force
            Black
            Spirit
                 talking & finding   in the dim   'Thou'
the forest   the   bullet   the   eye   of   rimmed
            meaning   & So threatening &
                        pressing

                from where the world filled   Sound!
            Speech/long sparking   the roots beside
                        the Heart!

                                    & the nut
                                    & the gear
                                    & the knuckle
                                    & the
            knife!   the stick!   the box of blood
                                    the hill suffused with
                                    star-Voice!

    & then what pressed into human life   bulging
            six Urges!   beautiful revealing &
                listening!   & 8 darknesses
                    burn & chant!

        I Suck Metal!   I put
                        Lead on my
                        Head
                        I drop oil
                        on my
                        Soil
                            I whisper I

am Wild-woman I hear
                    that robbers
            see visions   of   crowning
    possibilities!
                    so soft
                    Radio what
                    is Witness
                    what smells
                    Floor wax
                    what hears
                    I.B. mussel

Hey, Vat means ziz technical brotherhoog?

Wild-Man & the Rhythm of the Mechanized System

who belongs   Devout
thousand rebirths   mix
a few seeds
three days
thick at the top
how do these plants digest   in full Sun/

6 submarines
fast frigates
1 battalion   one onion
12 fast roses & a shower of s p e e d i n g
meteors   1 reconnaissance squadron   15 minesweepers

helpless in
the line of duty a
man dies
head sticking out of cement
/it's a thrilling once-in-a-lifetime
spectacle!
suck rubber & chop timber
/steel plants & the coming
Afrikanization of 12 hens & 24 cheeses/ O Boy!

a man with ideas
& a man whistling
in the light/tyme
of revolution
& bloody experience/

What about the
equipment
what about the fish   throw them back in the Sea

                    while the
                      gap
                     could
                     lead
                      to
                Fearing Things

        O Motor Vehicle
        O Radio Station
        O Meat & Wool
     O Major Airline
                        O Sacred Mechanized
                        System o' bliss!

Wild-Man & the Contemplation of Lunar Incest

there's almost NO LIMIT
to thinking in terms of miscellaneous Blood Groupings

WILD-MAN!
WYLD-MAYN!
WILDE-MAHN!
WHILD-MANE!

& so to radio-iodide
multi-movements & shortness
clear causes/ culture in
artificial energy fueling,   excess
of grueling unknown streaming blood conditions

V I V A   W I L D - M A N !

do the eyes look strange to you? then check

the mother
is she Sicilian?
Felonious intercourse/ sure quick vomit fast!

in case of rape
in case of incest
in case of
black & blue veins
do you smell
strange aromas?   Lunar highlands
O neutral metals

the planets are large & the surfaces
furious   the forces of the thick atmosphere

spring bigly   & cause minor

109

night sweating   of animals & friendly
injuns   Animal Bites!

romance of the rose
the christian mystics the hydraulic
press & reverence & gas engines & iron
lungen   burning your Bunsen!
fract/uring your calculating
machine!
So sweet

The Organization in the Jungle

10,000 times   the
circuit   with largest   bunch of violets
the 7.1% common fraction of life   the forces produce
white & purple
influences
of power   To call

the landscape   grand flow

the earth
is farmland the
ceremonial palaces croak Sexual Attraction

the part
the microwave tapers
gravitation
natural sections

/Territory is scenic beauty so
killing/ly rare

the hope is the

loose mad exile   to begin
to leave   the wave of
secrets
which despite
the spears
rule the
lowest in the world

is noise cropping up
the head of the sheep
waves in jungle growth
The area extends below 60 degrees S.

the disputed islands in the South

                              theocratic worms
                    fill up   in the hot & dry
              lunatik desert   .the heaven
        drops glass
& rust
                    Wild-Man chews a blade of grass.

The Mystery of Wild-Woman & the Perfect Peace

```
                    floods     point     the
      westward migration           reproduce the
                                    extra
                                    energy

reconvert it      to SOUTHWESTERN ASIA      AFRIKA

                    memory of the
            Attraction of a celestial body for
                        Zero

physical change of      mantowoman      wild-woman
                    the catalyst of change/

                    GREAT!
                              call the manifestation
      vision receiver      Rare-Earth

                                    it
                                    continues
                                    to
                                    end
                                    for
                                    him/
                                    wild-
                                    woman
                                    Saviour
                                    of
                                    Juice

  & the land is luxuriant             fragrant
                                    with
                                    voodoo
            excess of bloodshed
```

                    rose in a
                    prime womb/ a
              trembling hydrogen bomb sweet
              mucous & texturous
         Sacred design
                    throughout &
    swarming everywhere the sucking bees the food juice
turning to her blood/her peace, perfect peace

                         Time
         cuts back
                to
              Her power   flat rock

Wild-Woman & the Thinking-on of Putrefaction

                              the subsoil in
                the territory
& birds were found living   the binding power
              was joyful

                          now Woman has thrown
          the scientific cowardice   the
        mocking forbidden

                          street
                          sewer
                              the distant backdrop
Divine service   the matter
                          of the
                          skin
                              the sun between the

                  spine
                  bones
                          wonder of unknown cause

generation of the nucleus/
                      the TOTAL MASS

                              to bombing &
                              construction
              an eagle flies over
        the ravages   of Frozen waste   & disappears
to warm regions

                              the approach
                              to home &
                              the land
                              the wealth

                    of Great Rivers
                    the winging
                    System
                    readily
                    exploitable
        made into desert (interior)

                    vileness in industry
                    consumption in Pacific
                    Ocean   a hostile
                    climate   makes birds
    sluggish

Wild-Woman & the Device of Mangling

                      leaving behind
            the animals   breakdown of
    the beginning   the judgement of separation
                 until the death &
sacrifice   the

            cuts of Rolled Iron and
                   Steel Products the
                   chemicals &
                   Power Machinery
                   metallurgy   the lunatik
    National Anthem   forces .   anathema

                           slow sigh .
                        hiss . slooc . soo .
                   gsp.

                   I fix my attention on
        A skeleton   reconciliation between particles &
ME   I suggest the
                   value of
                   weakness   to go to bed
                                     without undressing
                                     and move the lever
                                     deal in cattle
          whisk   away   the
                   human form   I Am A Wonder Worker
                                  I glance at others' eyes
                                  I appear with wings and
                                  a striking-fast switch-
                                blade

                           I smash
          obstructions

117

                    I cause acid to eat any
            sort of hope
                              I dry up
                        the wetness of plants
                  I hold a device
              and . mangle
          it is the day of . derision

The Equinox Commandment

I glance with
        the   EYE   nothing is
    quiet   O no idleness   the parasite is
   laughing   we are anesthetized &
  free   of thrilling   what is brought to a
     level   of peace?
what is white derangement?   who carried the young
     backwards to travail?
               the mother strips
      the corn-husk   she gives the child
    the bone of the world
           with a steel nail
       a comma is etched it is
       a pause on the child's
      heart
              except each other
      with abundant   ball-to-leg   grief
  we are cooking with
love   the brown grain
     numbers billions in our
    brain
               I am going eastward
        for a meal with-
         out Anger   my spirit
      is Untouched &
     Breathing
            a green Parrot
   a thousand years long-living speaks
  my stage-
directions   I will not plunder
      with a sword of
     crazy steel

            my energy will
        spring   & disperse in my
    holy   self
                                        my compassion
                            is sun   gleaming &
                        eternal
                    where is
                the warmth

from The Joe Chronicles   Part 2

1979

King Lugalannemundu Also from the Cruel Cube Derived and/or Betrayed

Origins the Soldier's breastplate
becomes   worse. Dry.   An enemy   Where King

Lugalannemundu

His abundant drink-offering His Eye
                                                            seeks
& S P A R E S   the hidden
                                                                victim

little woman in Thessaly   idolatry the
sitting on a hill   Ice which lies
sees Fallen down   combined and laid
a person and her palm o'   across the surface
the hand holds a   the people remember
collection of elements   the committed junk
she sits on the   the borne up
throne, her yellow   Noah's ark
whining parakeet   in midday on all
names in healing   fours that myth
the earliest hope   plucks its skin
THE NAME   & descends
of some undetermined   with noiseless
animal   shrieks

miss mary is languid
today the parakeet pale-red
legs tap along with her one thumb-
nayl

the clay and blood
                        comes & blends

there is a problem
like the sea
the FOOT
of the bird
crumbles to   dust.

organized space & time

and another piece of meat King Lugalannemundu
signaled
    to eat & become primordial.
       primordial.
            a reward
  where one laughed like a cat does, beloved.
       the paws
      rubbing & tearing
   rotating wide. the sky
         the grin of
the cat is shaped like a wheel.
      the close-cropped
    pestilence
   calm
   slaughter
   the violet eye
   yielding up
Straight striking the Sun /backward

        it could
     be the same
    word.
   used again like the meat
  blackens
with Age. heroic. holy monotonous
history
   re-shaped
   because   I desire
the dregs of the believer prone to joy
& anger
   the intestinal sickle-shaped
    dance
     a whirlwind fist
  which is certainly itself

125

the cows owned
by King Lugalannemundu
his words
influenced by
bombardments
of flame.

                    I Sanction and plead
                    to the wooden forma
                    tion
the formulae
that shadowed the
Nether World.
                    oy Gevalt
                    Go' Bless
                    shake your ol'
                    Real Thing
                    Sing & Throw
                    clusters of
                    Monkey-roses
                    Owe thyself
                    to the inter-
                    ception of
                    Rays of bright
                    favorable lang-
                    uage
        the Just serenity of
        Phantasmal prayer
        Slightly Acid the
        Power of One emotion
        the Harmony of your
        Melody & Smooth
        Time.

get thru said the light send Magic on, between Almost
        Name the True State detonating device Yod
                            Power
                            Blowing the fuse
                            burnished morning-
                            glory the
                            failure & Wisdom

                              Vain for us
                              Beneficial to
                              the face above My
                              axis
                    Swiftly she Walks
                    & is gone.

the breath
in King Lugalannemundu's
throat.

                Night Only the night accepts
the Masculine intermingling
            a Punch & Judy show, the night of
    Double Awareness   that episode
                devastated King
        Lugalannemundu
        his red scrotum
      the section of
    his Travail   belief for knowledge
                    choose! choose!

        I grant
        we will
        confirm
        transform
        the sign
        the dedi-
        cation
        the step
        by the dog's
        tooth the
        wilderness
        the normal
        drawing fate
        into view the
        bad egg
        miraculous   first time adventure
                            the meaning leaving
                            Space Seed Fish Hook
                            Opening Poem the crest
                            to nothing possible
                            blooming 100 beautiful
                            Visions go slow Some

Mystical singing imm-
easurable you hear
while you live
That's great.

like us.
LIKE US. The perfect King.

                    his Anthem Was
        I got a lotta Nerve for you.
                              the preference
of the Heart/   the Song of His Story of
            courage   the Soldier's Blue
                           handkerchief
                           Waving in the
                           Rain.   I am the One-
        Eyed child
        my dark metal lips
        Form a Vow/   in the afternoon
                       I crave a glass
                       a glass of wine
                       Sharp as
        vinegar   I'm wide-awake Now/ & my First Step
        is
All-Meaningful   from a source
                         of shining always
                         the secret face
                         trembles with
                         laughter the
                         brown worms
                         measure the
                         distance
        Bird's wing.
                              butcher-shop King
                              he knocks against
                              the scarecrow, tends
                              to speak Japanese
        says, Super
              Destruction
              a doubtful
              horror   I bewail the truth
                        pregnant with

Separation
I would Have you
Die for me
like a Swahili
you would Swallow
your scream &
stand still
here & there
my Prophecy would
Make you sweat.

Lugalannemundu, He Sends a Letter

                        Dear Dehumanizing
                        Dear Woman
what is good?
                    Look!   Spread the contours
                of the brain backward

                O Fish when will you find God?
when will you find
God?

                        Downward
                        the tits of the
                        Angel of Death

                                the False God's secret
                                Air the consuming
                                Question

                        Dear fiend
                        Dear uncircumcised   One.

                        Oh Child What is Good?

                        The Question remains
                        on this point

                        At the center of the

                                Deplorable machine
At the center
Dear Hell
                    deplorable machine
                                        Help
                        the tits of the
                        Angel of Death
                        Evil Yezer   Help

133

art or humanity

old-fashioned propa/ganda.

signed your friend
King Lugalannemundu

The King & the Greek Woman in the Shopping Center

King Lugalannemundu in
Gimbels
the smell my
fervor   I make no Triumph Twice   explain
& exult   my
restoration   my feeling of the faythful Smile

I go anywhere   My fervor
my American tribal chant   my oxygen
my fervor
who arranges the book

My Song?   my oxy-
gen
my res-
toration   I smile today.

yr/ Eyes reveal King Lugalannemundu

do you know
that I am lifted to
something
agony   that wheels so many
things

that the pure inquisitive
the eye sees
Origins
in midday
the hope
drink-offering

          with itself
          the backward calm
          signal
          the primordial
          flame

     I ask aloud
     the Earth's crust
     a Foot above/   joy

he said

THE KING

little

woman in Thessaly

languid the bird
in organ-
ized space the guyanese king he said Power in
the striped prison uniform the bird in space
organized like the
foot   the Soldier's
breastplate
descend the earliest

hope

sit across

from me

miss mary   be languid like the
foot of a
bird
the steady drive belonging a
storm
backward

the grin of
King Lugalannemundu

from the cruel cube
derived with

the wheel the whirlwind
fist

                    I See the guyanese
          king   with noiseless
cries   fallen down   dealing
               the bro-ken
          spir-it dead-tired &

          WITH THE Word the
          downpour

                         imitation
                         the right of
                         the body to
          bend

          into electric
          Skin

          sit across
          from me

          the Noah's ark
          of your bones
          pleases me

          I remember first
          your nose-jewel
          glinting

          like the ruby-rain-blood
          of the crucifix

          sit across
          from me

& the heart
will tremble

from the grin
of King Lugalannemundu

from Shemuel

1979

      he hit her in the churning
body
          she hit him in the worried
                      body
        he hadn't earned a nickle in
   a week   why should she take
   the loafer's shit
          in belfast she hit
      him in the churning stomach
in dublin he hit her in the
                 pregnant
body
       it has become a way of life
    he a strongman hitting she a
  strongwoman hitting
  they tell the medes you don't understand
        our ways

the soldier
& the sailor
& the crater
& the muddy
rocks & the
monsoon rain
& the large
house without
a garden of
onions let
alone a cucumber
through the
deserted village
you can hear
the unborn cucumbers
& onions crying
the sobs say again
& again everything
o everything is gone.

the back shadow idol
in the back alley of uz

you of the back alley your
shadow idol is in back of you

you of backs & shadow idols in
the back alley of fetid uz

uz is a stinking fetid alley you
follow the shadows of your idols

your idols shadow you in uz &
everywhere you are in the back

uz shadows you uz makes you forever
fetid the back alley of shadows follow

you are fetid follow fetidness your
back alleys stink & everywhere you

are in the alley of backness uz will
not save you your idols shadow you

across the river

no-feathered

birds missing primary & secondary feathers

swollen feet

abandoned pesticide horrible residue

obviously

polychlorinated biphenyls

world's oceans

obviously   breakdown   obviously   breakdown

hate health

the great gulls

sewage   obviously   midway

between weekend visits

is of significance

obviously

hate god

hate god

make more breakdown

obviously

she gave him a camera
he gave her an afternoon opera
she wrote down the words
of the fisherman of gaza

he thought of the fogbound
grin
she wondered about
agony he moved 20 pounds of
complicated neutrality
she danced in a
minor dance group in uz
he liked the extraordinary lighting of
uz
she slightly shifted her reasons
for liking uz
he pondered on her churning
body she hit him in the child sound

he hit her in
the curling body
she hit him in the
purple heart
he cocked his
wallet at her face
she stuck
her pencil at his
function
she hit him in
the churning body he hit her
in the troubled heart
she hit him
in the velvet balls
he hit her
in the plate-glass
womb
in dublin town

became
        known
    absolving
                    she hit him
    in the corrupt body
became known
                fully cursing
    he hit her in the
scary eye
                absolving
    faster than a
whoring son of mr. yin
                        faster than a
        fly eats honey
    absolving
            within the letter
        the spirit of the
    law

                    he hit her in the
               churning body
                                        she hit him in
                    the knocking body   he hit her
               earth/ she hit him
                                        behind the breast-rib
          he hit her singing
                              mouth
                    she snuck up
               behind the nose-rings
                                        behind the apples/
                              she crawled   like snotting
                              samael after spewing
          onan   then she hit him thenshehithim
          in the python ventricle/ of his rotting
being   then even the rusted nail
               or the cursing of sarah
          or the scorn of ishmael couldn't
          draw the angel of death near

for Jerome Rothenberg

let pale hand of
infamous canaanite
lo eighty hands steal
a bony thumb out of
new york door-locks &
let the eighty hands
of canaanites seek a
redemption & let them
kill the evil yezer
that modifies my words
So that the words—Let no gods before me be worshipped—
shift & twist & slant &
alter to—Worship a hundred gods before
me
& tho i bend my knee to
moloch
i am righteous & saved

from Constructs

1985

Tension

Consciously or unconsciously
the act of tensing a muscle
has a tendency to occupy the brain/
stubby/foiling/the
fly in the ointment so to speak
with an inviolable strain/
thus the sequence of thoughts
pushing into art forms from out
the exploration and skill
of fixed space focused from out
of the pull of straining
forearms think of the rigid
fingers of St. Joan of Arc
even fishermen or Simone Weil
pushing into their sides
the passion a device as useful
as a steel plate in the skull
of a woman resolute and sitting
down near a tree or a shrub
contemplating the split/second
when her calf muscle
cramped perversely making
the woman lose her balance and
falling from the ladder the month
before/an image in her mind
of the sinews of cats tensing/
hunting

Winters North

Plates   space   headfirst plates earth
sandbanks   twotone   amount of red in
legs of dancer-birds resemblance of my
energies   the corneas   delighted girl-
child   the glass shiny round motion to
the   girl-child   the first winter of
pre-set depth   dimensions   of the wooden
rocking horse   the end of wintertime photo-
graph of the eye seeing the leaning mando-
lin   all around the house inside outside
broken pumice in two places   the first
forms delighting smiling girl-child

The Wood Fence

this indispensable you need your
project if it grows older you stick
it into the illustrated guide with
a grain of salt you take history and
character size yourself up make a
microscopic assumption time immemorial
says you're right once learn one thing
at a hundred times seven sags down the
old poet's eye-lid when it rains and
you have no coat on the old farm fence
props itself up on the scarecrow   I
lie absorbing the sun lying on my hand

Chariots in Subways

oscillated   insect diverting the attention
and it astonishes   the interruption of
the image descending the stairs of the
subway   where no wood sawed   the sole
traveler simply my own motion glorious
chariots of a classical epoch where under
the eyelids sit girls fighting and
wrestling the flat metal of their perfect
wrists the enamel of the fingernails
giving stern challenge to the ages coming
lofty nobility omnipotent they will stand
for truths stranded on the first sandy beaches

Plywood the Hammer Too

accept into the other part in other
in space the slender deer stretches a
leg surface smooth in some cases while
you hammer you see nothing but the simple
woven wire the tools in the corner bring
your eyeglasses round the top keep the
image of the deer's round mouth the
hinge of the jaws as a frame of 2 by 4's
below your heel scrapes the cardboard box
you used yesterday it was a good idea to
keep dust dirt out no need to nail it down
let the deer have a look

from W.C. Fields in French Light

1986

She fell back
the warped one
He drew circles
She died at the hands
of fifty warriors
The army saw them
at Sacre Cœur
They joined her
up at the hill
like a flock o' birds
over Sacre Cœur

Two calluses a day
on my one foot,
a coral reef hard
as food production
in undeveloped nations,
a potential source
of tiny sea animals
plankton

I'll learn how
to say Sacre Cœur
perfectly like beans
cooking in a pot
of black iron
My voice will be
wonderful
I'll develop patterns,
flux & structures
It will be marvelous
photo-regulation,
a respiratory metabolism
that is the rosy

perfection of two hours
of my life every week
learning french
entertaining myself
at a meeting of
acid-rain analyzers
& sliding on the floors
in the perfumed casbah
of Sacre Cœur O
Sacre Cœur O
Cœur O Sacre

Yearning
for good rabbit-meat
the elite Egyptian
in low tones
explains the conversations
of Algerians
who rue the day
they left that inhibited
dusty town outside of
Algiers

Who rue the day
they left their
inhibited dusty town
to strike out!
O hometowns of no
rabbit stew
and the wrath of oil-kingdoms
triple-edged electric signs

And W.C. said:
Listen to my jargon
I like to look at you
The lure of your
arched nostrils
captures me
When you are in

the process of purifying
yourself
with blue bathoil
the logic of the world
is in the color
of the rhythm
of your hands

When you thieve
my money-belt
I absorb the electricity
of the movements,
your stereo-sinews
don't let me down

As for poetry
I greatly admire
W.C. Williams
and his two flossies
for the price of one
Two flossies for the price
of a good doctor-poet
a good doctor of boyish
charm is worth a festival
of flossies
A gaggle of girls
in a state of ecstasy
female dementia
described by compassionate
doctor
   What has the name
    of a dog
   Whistles asthmatically
    and does capers?
   And makes the best
    cabbage salad in town
   And makes the best
    cabbage salad in town
   Patterns

Of patronized women

The dramatic blood
combining the letters
moving forward
the penetrated cells
the bony lower jaw
in pure line split
like a wax crayon
In the absence
of searching
I could've danced
all night
Dancing the way I think
Bursts forces coincidence
My voice does not exist
outside of amazement!

A sandworm emerging

This is a hundred yard
dash
I am racing the alphabet
I am calling myself
in a loud voice
I lay hidden in a
southern delta
Expelled like a
placenta
I squirm to see
Sacre Cœur
The next day
all comes to pass
In an hour I predict
desire
This wisdom is ordinary,
visible
Day, week, month
Innocent as an
explanation

I wonder about oil,
the manufacturing of
whalebone girdles
that women in the 19th
century wore
I think about their
sweat, knuckles
rubbing, imprints on
the hips
Various as signs of
the zodiac

A crisis waits near
an ulcerated leg
It is finished
It causes caseworkers
to venture beyond the
call of duty
To astonish themselves
to survey the decay

I will move
over the sand
A solution is
my next impulse
A sandworm emerging
again & again
Fission breaking
The principle of
combinations
Elements dangerous
Mental crucibles
Striking fire
Pearls in my glowing
hands

I remember the woman
in mutton-sleeves who
breathed scalding steam
The rare earth she walked
Passion, laughter,
angular jaw, sufi smile
Eyes of Mona Lisa
She meditated on fuel
shortage, a way to
lighten the load
Would you spend money
on a ruptured camel?

To wind up at the bend
of a crater

the cargo buried
in sand

Wrapping it up in Montmartre
A haunting mosaic of
sensations, algerian meat-pies
a country road
an ambitious motor accident
The blood on the tall
dead grass forming
circles, crickets eating
Yellow flowers
Balancing & singing
A nerve in the body
of Sacre Cœur
The shock absorbed into
the pine trees, triangles
Highest intensity
Crashing cymbals
"Pull down thy vanity"
Elements of structure

Who wanders like
inner bloom
evokes the brown evening
Extends alone
Intensifies eighth black
distance
Questions the round
liquid moon

The bloodstream loves
the rectangle
Power of voice
catching breath

Hawk in the nest
I can tell the bird is shy
Inject hawk with dioxide
no limit

Morning back
Feeding time in the
wilderness
Circling claws at the sky

And W.C. said,
O O those french boys
from the gulf of Arabia O
Blue-nippled women
from Japan, America, Sweden
O those infra-red leers O
Monsters, assassins O
Clowns of happiness
where no dogs barked O
old nobody breathe
on Sacre Cœur

I am a whore
wearing a hat
with oriental frankincense
and money tucked
in the seams
I am a poet and black ravens
swirl over me
I am a singing sailor in jail
I am a poor cowboy
at 12 o'clock high
One eye is filled
with melodrama
Would you break bread
with me and listen to my songs?

Beethoven heaves and splits open
Women in the wilderness
The south bronx agonizes
Rhythm and winter solstice
thunderous in the brain
Ear sucks up staggering noise
The labyrinth of my arteries
curving to Sacre Cœur

In the autumn of
William Carlos Williams
sweet-heart of America
brought forth
the two-headed calf

I remember the wedding
of the doctor to the girl
The poet to the kissing-
hugging minx

One good doctor with boyish
charm is worth a festival
of flossies

Two for the price of one
A question of imitation
A state of perpetual ecstasy

What has the name of a dog
and does capers
I remember the whirling
many-colored coat
of doctor Bill

Two women for the price
of one good doctor-poet
William Carlos Williams

My manure-caked booted
foot kicking the tongue-
depressors clear

And makes the best

fruit-salad in town
And makes the best
fruit-salad in town

Sweetheart of America
metamorphosis of aleph-bet

Clear up his ass
Gusts of breeze over the hill

I saw her a gentle wife
giving a straight answer
to doctor Bill
She calculates his tax assets
and would have died
for him too
        Patterns
        Of humiliated women
            I see the beautiful
            colors in the globs
        of oil in the gutter
        How I see them O
            I acquaint my eye
            to the new
        architecture,
        said the guru
            of machismo
            I would like
        to screw you so
I live where you are
where you are going
where you cannot go it alone

Alone the lonely poet
lonely as a fish
speaks into the darkness
in the voice of W.C.:
O my god we can hunt
the lions down
on a rainy afternoon

Who do you have to talk to?
Only me
And I am always the dead weight
tugging at your Japanese
eyelids

Flossie, do the ravenous
knitting that women do
Flossie, do your kind o' thing,
          cook the pork-roast
          move that rear-end
Say kindly ever kindly:
I ponder on the residue of tea,
the spontaneous gods of Anu,
Enlil and Enki
My kisses shifting
to the male nipples
of my beloved doctor Bill

I am Flossie speaking,
Doctor Williams' wife
He never knew that I
was not a french woman
Dear Bill, dear
you did not know
that I was not french

See Bill, the kingdom
of women who have a
fixed character O
they strike matches
on your head
and watch you burn

Sacre Cœur needs oil
Sacre Cœur is in france
& needs precious oil
La belle france
needs to gulp down oil

needs to gulp down oil
needs to gulp down oil

Memory of my body
patterns, power of shadows
forms integrating
primary material of self
liking the shapes
avoiding the void
form the form of shadows
makes
a line between the light
& darkness & light &
darkness
the continuum of time
the shadows & light
the patterns mingling

Each woman has a stick
to bang on a drum
& in sharp daylight O
takes your two legs twisted
seizes your chin
smooth as an onion
& the women call you
to question O
& the women call you
to question O

Alone the lonely poet
lonely as a fish
speaks into the darkness
in the voice of W.C. Fields:
& were your feet swollen up
m'dear & were they swollen up
m'dear
Well, let me purge 'em m'dear
Well, let me purge 'em

My hunger has mercy

when I finally
overtake the four days
of my life
that I put
on the butcher's block
I have been roped in
like a calf
by the executioner

Beloved doctor Bill
is flashing like the sign
McDonald's cooks with wine
Essence to essence he's
pilfering flossie's jewel box,
burrowing like an ant
into the tucks of rayon velvet
His orgasm floats like mist
in an english garden, says the
poet in the darkness

Forward
the penetrated cell
moving, drawing hidden
information, mystery of
albumen, glistening like
a flirting man's black eyes
I could have danced all night

from How Much Paint Does the Painting Need

1988

And I gave my brief turbulent   mad genius legend
& tragic life idealization   my colorful palette
megalithic anxiety   I PAINT   I PAINT
frenzied activity   seizures   I tried to preach
to oppressed mining families   I mutilated my left
ear   ecstatic sunflowers   I lucid Vincent
I paint   I paint   every inch I felt force
my brief mutilated life   the area of my ear   the
light year   every second pressure   fractions
of my rhythmic ecstacy   my small lucid eyes sweetly
expressive   after the cutting   such frenzied
activity in Arles   but not for trivial
things   my wavelike nature   a searching megalithic
anxiety   my colorful palette   my small lucid
eyes sweetly expressive

She was susceptible   she hooked her neck forward
the passionate Polonaise   the edges of her nostrils fiery
She was susceptible to remembrances   O it's going to be
murder at Christmastime for me   my blood pressure
dropped to a dangerous level   eyelids of black glass
wanting to tango   the roots of trees   are my tormentors
waiting   staring   with eyelids of pale jade   a sliver of
glass   She was susceptible to remembrances   of wanting
an artery to bleed   the muscles & tendons of my
calves bunch like onions tied with string   of lying close
of loving hot water   of the effect on her cells
on her nerves

She hooks her head   to the side   listening
like a parrot   perched on a wash basin
& a tank with a spigot   & a mass of metal cast
leavings   She's staring through   a spiral
construction   the blood is dripping
intersecting circles   on the canvas   She's applying
pressure   to the artery   with a long
tapering finger

Saud said: Once upon a time the association
of a woman weaving had a predictable magical power
coldness & darkness of the Gothic soul   as clear as notes
in an orchestral score   coldness & darkness   Saud said:
The rational order collides with a spontaneous discharge
of sperm & sweat   mutilated bodies disposed on
the canvas of Guernica   ejaculatory material of excited
colors   black bull of pain   Saud said

She was susceptible to remembrances
black liquid shoe polish   of having once only been the
affectionate Polonaise   I feel the presence of eyelids of
black glass loose scales   I prowl & wander with half-closed
eyelids   I make a snorting sound   I would have liked
to have told T.S. Eliot to stick his head in the toilet
A large patch of scalp   She was susceptible
to remembrances   where is the chronological point of
western civilization   was he to have come to dinner   are my
tormentors at the edges   to flounder   to bleed
to rot   off foreign shores   to forget   that she sentenced
him to bleed   to stare

She said   I want to paint   an anonymous woman
& a naked horseman   The face spreading out   as the paint
feeds on it   minute amounts of displacement
a dark & nervous atmosphere   a flickering light
becoming sharper   I taste the paint edging between
my teeth   Saud said   See the edge   vanishing spreading
becoming smaller   A fault in the canvas   as
the paint feeds   on the stretched membrane   darkening
the Gothic soul   my lips taste bitter   I want
the paint to invade   the lurid flickering brush
through which   my own life-blood flows

Saud said: The Virgin & Child depicted even as doodles
on the computer   reverberate in a myriad of bloody colors &
banishes   the coldness & darkness   destroying
the worm in your heart   Saud said: Coldness & darkness of
the Gothic soul   methodical dead material   copious
adoration of kith & kin   honors the rational
order   My elbows wing out   escaping the coldness
& darkness of the Gothic soul   Saud said

She feels   the urge   to rattle the doorknob
it is locked   she steps backwards   examining the scratches
the peeling paint   configurations   whorls of circles
decaying wood   Through the action of her eyes
the door evolves   into a canvas of rhythmic movement
She feels   the urge to step forward   bracing
her toes against the door   look into
the window   study the body of T.S. Eliot who is
half-dead   half-rotten   half-shattered
on the bed   in the sunny afternoon

179

Her ovaries   are mother-of-pearl
said Saud   her smile   a shower   is a shower
of golden monkeys   embroidered   on
green linen   Inside her body   a dawning
a mystery   nestling   in clusters
of sequins & seed-pearls   Saud said
Tant le désir   weeping   weeping
sweet tears   sanctified ivory
thighs   that conquered
Rome   A circular configuration
of tiny polished shells
gleams   on the crown   of her noble head
from which ringlets   of blonde silk
are suspended

Saud said: The dark iridescent head
of the Virgin & Child   is concealed   by a blank wall
She feels the urge   to duck behind   to lock
herself in behind the spirals of peeling
paint & rotting wood   The Queen of Heaven lurks
in back of crumbling plaster   her hands have been
cut off   & replaced by silver ones   the Child
is clutching   a long tapering finger
I feel   a vicious itch   above my tailbone
too difficult to reach

Devils Clowns & Women

I was the one   who found you   who brought
you to America   I was wearing   red silk   when you
   brought me to America   I was wearing a white cotton
         dirndl   that you had made   you always
                  gave special care   to me
in the evening   you would read to me   I remember
the small hotel   on top of a mountain
               where we spent a night   we watched
the sunrise with the sun shining   on the mountain top
         while the country down   below   was still
                  in darkness
      I remember
               that white dirndl that I made
for you   it had lace   lace is so inviting to the touch
      the texture of rounded edges   so pleasing
fifty years ago   society ladies   displayed their
               collections   on gilt-edged boards
a popular tea-time diversion   Tanya wore black lace
         her skin   luminous   even the jasmine
flowers become dull compared to her skin   wouldn't
   you like to be alone with her   and take all
                        her   clothes off
               nourished by the purity of childlike
   beauty
         you'd like to photograph Tanya   wouldn't you
               you'd have as much control over yourself
      as a moth flying   around   a   candle
                  As long as you kept a camera
in your hands   you'd be safe   Tanya is every
                  red-blooded man's dream
      where is she?   did you see her?   you said vicious
   things to her   you have an ugly heart
                     it was night-time   she
couldn't see the look   on my face   tucked away

in a far corner   of my brain lie the
soft tender feelings   I stand in horror   of them
wind-swept deserts
and gypsy caravans   that's what Tanya brings to mind
delicious in white
I want to take Tanya   for a day of swimming
in the countryside
hello   hello   my darling girl
she'll come to me   we'll watch the trees   breathe
I'll hand her an orange
she'll eat it   pulp & rind   we'll let desire run into
our bodies   she will not be a cold girl
she will not want to miss out   on any   of my stories
You know   when I first met her
I knew she was a rare woman   she moved
like an athlete   strong firm legs   I
was resigned   detached   Well   you've got your girl
I'll teach you how to cook
a traditional Sunday dinner   succulent roast
beef   you will wallow in envy   In Thailand   when you
kissed me   you told me that the soft space
above the corner of my lips was
shockingly erotic   I'm just a carcass of evil
next to you   let me comb your hair
the miracle of you
is unequaled after a thousand years   I am part
of a long migration of fearless lesbians hardly
ever recognized   except as the witch
in fairytales   concocting
potions of flowing menstrual
blood   eating young virgins
You excite me   your hunger
your yearnings   happy now?   You're
a sleeping beauty
But I am all tangled impulses
I am not detached   You and I in every
pose   sexual tender   our hands and teeth
our noses   close together   And I will hold
your curving body   taut with desire

182

                              We should sing praises
                to the loveliness of young girls   Queens
            and their daughters   we don't know where
         we are going to die   sacred responsibilities
    to give care   & protect
                       In Thailand   you accused me
    of trying to blind you   you had gotten an eyelash in your
         eye   under the lower lid   you were trying
    to remove it   I went over to help you   while
       I was moving your eyelid up and down   gently
                 to dislodge the eyelash
    you said   don't stand behind me   I don't like to
             feel only a presence
                          I have bad nerves   there's a
    head-on fiery battle   In a poor land   I longed
         for you   for want of your fair   hand   as a little
      girl I gathered spring flowers for the monks   for
    spite I hid a chicken head in a bouquet
                            the monk's reaction made me numb
           cold   distorted   he simply said   I see it all
     I see everything   you're a little
                             butterfly
          I take you with a grain
                     of salt
                I take each step as if it was
    the last   to avoid the falsity   as best I can
       no matter what its form   woman like
                fire & water makes   the truth live
                     within herself

             What did he do?
             He made a pass at me
             O he did did he?
             What did he do?
             Did he whistle at ya?
             He oggled me
             Oggled you? I thought
             maybe he diddled you
             You know when he first

                         183

saw you he asked me
if you were the wife
He didn't say is she your wife?
He said is she the wife?
He said that you looked like
a hot piece
                    Roses whose haunting beauty
echoes thy lips   you have the dirtiest mouth
    of any woman that I've ever seen

            She is my sole source   to feel her is
to feel a snarl   of honeysuckle   sometimes to annoy me
    she would tap her foot incessantly   I would
        grab her knee under the table   holding her leg
            down   we played a game   she'd hoist
me up with her feet   she'd lie on her back   brace
            her feet against my thighs and fly
                        me through the air   and the light
    scattering around her hair   sweet rituals

            What did she wear?   What was her face like?
Her hair?   Her body?   Proud   strong   she wore a black
lace dress   a twisted coal-black bead choker   bright
        blue beads   the night I was with her
after dessert   when coffee was served   He reached inside
    his jacket and withdrew a cigar   the whore reached
        across the table and took   it from him
He smiled   she bit off the end of the cigar with slightly
        parted lips   exposing white teeth   moistened it
            with the tip   of her tongue   and slowly
lit it   She threw back her head   and blew smoke
                toward the ceiling
                        a binge with a whore
        with childlike beauty
                    I'll tuck a patchwork quilt   around you
we'll drink steaming mugs of   hot buttered rum
                        what could be more cozy
        than that?
                    you should pile   your hair

                        184

atop your head   so that it falls   in beguiling tendrils
   around the nape   of your sweet neck   you look
so wan   so tragic   let me help you slip   into
   the silk kimono that   I bought for you   from   Thailand

                    Just when you think
                    that she is your pal
                    you look for her
                    and find her hangin'
                    'round some other gal
                    what were you when
                    I found you
                    a gal whose arteries
                    and veins are made
                    of rusty wire and sticky
                    eggshells
                    convicted of drug smuggling
                    burglary and murder

      I eat the same food   that the inmates eat   I sleep
where they sleep   I hold them   they walk by the
guards   at the iron gate   a prisoner with tattoos from
                    her neck to her waist   she pulls up
      her skirt   and shows me a scar   on her abdomen
            she asks me   if I can get her some   medicine
another prisoner pulls down her lower lip   and requests
   special bridgework   another asks me for warm milk
                    I calm them   and listen
                                to them cry
            they tell me their names   aliases   and crimes
               there was   a little girl   who had a
                          little curl right in the
         middle of her face
                    According to Benjamin Franklin
                    there are only three faithful
                    things   an old wife   an old dog
                    and ready money
                    leave things the way they are
                    quoth the Lord of battle

chieftain   mercenary   sorcerer
street commando   gangster daddy
Doc Holliday

She takes me for granted
I'm too too generous   with her   I don't know why
she rips up my needlepoint   years ago   she cut my belt
in half   it was navy-blue leather   she said she
needed a belt   she took it without   asking   I found
it later   she had cut a piece off
& punctured a hole into it   so it would fit around
her small waist
Tanya singing   her moist oval lips
like a Christmas caroler in the snow
Why couldn't I fall into   her arms   without
falling into her hands
What happened?

you got burned
She would sit   with me   for
hours   her hands resting   on her knees   attentive   sensitive
I loved her then
who loves the most   dear
no matter what her age
she'll have that skin   life is too short &
winter too long to go
without my darling girl

I was thinking of the photo
my mind drifts in and out
she was nude except for
a white mink coat draped
around her shoulders   fur
against her skin   she was
standing with her back
towards the camera   her
rump gleamed in the moonlight
her what?   her rump
body & soul   I love to dance
abandoned to dreams   legends   mysterious divinities

remembrances of silken touches   sunlight warm on
                    my breasts   the lacy
     butterfly at her bodice   quite a bit of gorgeous
ass   temptation abounds   the color   subtle   twilight
     lavender   come close   touch it   touch it
                    the trees   the gardens   the pool
          lovely soft warm colors   a cloud of dried
                    baby's breath

                    I hate autumn   the first chill
     my skin hurts   let's make a fire
                    you love the rust and gold
of trees   don't you?   I'm cold   my legs are cold
               I can't sleep   scrub the bathtub
I want to do it   because I can't sleep   it's three A.M.
               he stands on her grave
               his legs wide apart
               witch face witch face
               boar tusks protrude from
               her cheeks   mud & plant
               fibers leak from her
               nipples faces & forms
               of demons devils clowns
               women spooks spooks
     Tanya is splendid   Tanya's skin is taut   smoothed
to perfection   healthy   woman   matron   model
          of proper behavior   tawdry slut   buffoons that
make me laugh   ugly   I shit in her cunt   I will buy
     my stunning piece jewels for her   gleaming satin skin
               then cherish it   then cherish it
                    she harasses me   she is like a sack
of hate that stretches shifts & changes shape
                    mask   fetish   cult-figure   volcano
                              rock cunt
she was smiling   at me when I gave her the earrings
          of gold & diamonds   I carried her over
               the threshold of our new home
                         she's home   it takes
just a fraction of a breath   to say
                         home

Anthropologists at a Dinner Party

I was sitting next to a round-haunched anthropologist
I was at a dinner party of Pict descent
The academics were friendly a gigantic-buttocked academic
An American professor of Scottish ancestry
descended from pure Pict let me explain it
according to the dict A Pict was one of a mixed
they amalgamated with race of aborigines and
the Scots some of them aryan invaders who once
tend to look like Santa occupied Great Britain
Claus he was porcelain eyed and cherry-cheeked
he was studying American Indian people
he was worried that mixed blood people had impractical
races were opportunists schemes
he liked museum posters bright opaque bean-eyed
he was making money with a pure blood esophagus
he was rushing off after to help his second wife
the dinner party was over
the anthropologist was articulately explaining
ethical culture he said the new baby was
the beginning of a new litter

This poem ought to be read across, down

He informed me that mixed
to the Indian people
he was rushing off after a
anthropology professor
rushing off to help
they should stay bright
pure blood esophagus
anthropologist at a dinner
cherry nose descended from
race who once occupied
descended from aborigines
anthropologists investigate
parties marrying a second
a Pict is one of a mixed
once occupied Great Britain
Some of them tend to look
Santa Claus, rushing off
party, taking care of the
being part of the new litter
Scottish ancestry
articulately

blood people do a disservice
when they join white culture
dinner party given by another
who's of the female gender
his new wife with the baby
opaque bean-eyed with a
a gigantic-buttocked
party, porcelain-pink cheeks
Picts who are of a mixed
Great Britain and who were
and aryan invaders
rushing off after dinner
time according to the dict
race of aborigines who
who amalgamated with the
Scots an anthropology
professor after a dinner
baby who he described as
an American professor of
An anthropologist was
explaining

and up and down, and down and around.

A NOTE ON THE AUTHOR

ROCHELLE OWENS is an internationally recognized poet, playwright, and video artist. She has published sixteen books of poetry. A pioneer of the experimental off-Broadway theater movement, she has been the recipient of five *Village Voice* Obie Awards and Honors from the New York Drama Critics' Circle. She has also been the recipient of grants from The Solomon R. Guggenheim Foundation, The New York Creative Artists in Public Service program, The National Endowment for the Arts, and The Rockefeller Foundation. She has taught at Brown University, the University of California—San Diego, and the University of Oklahoma. She has lectured and read in the United States, France, and the United Kingdom. Her work has been translated into and performed in French, German, Italian, Spanish, Ukrainian, and Japanese.